CHRISTIAN WORSHIP

A THEOLOGICAL AND HISTORICAL INTRODUCTION

GLEN O'BRIEN

WIPF & STOCK · Eugene, Oregon

Wipf and Stock Publishers
199 W 8th Ave, Suite 3
Eugene, OR 97401

Christian Worship
A Theological and Historical Introduction
By OBrien, Glen
Copyright©2013 Morning Star Publishing
ISBN 13: 978-1-4982-3135-0
Publication date 5/29/2015
Previously published by Morning Star Publishing, 2013

For Professor Donald Boyd

CONTENTS

Preface by Professor Robert Gribben

When I was appointed to teach in 1998, I was asked to suggest an appropriate title for my professorial Chair. The result was 'Worship and Mission'. The idea really goes back to a Swiss Reformed theologian, Jean-Jacques von Allmen, whose book *Worship: its Theology and Practice* (Oxford, 1965) had made the connection between two fields often regarded as antithetical. In the same way as some people oppose 'evangelical' and 'ecumenical', so some set 'liturgy' and 'evangelism' against each other. Words soon become battle lines, if we do not listen to each other. Von Allmen (whom I knew in his old age) said the relationship of worship and mission was like the life-giving balance of *diastole* and *systole*, the two heart-beats which drive the blood throughout the body to feed it and draw it back through the lungs to refresh and purify it. The Church's mission must always be connected with its worship: we are not merely a society of do-gooders. The Church's worship must always issue in mission (evangelism and service), for we are not a society for the study of antique rituals. On the personal level, when we come to faith in Christ, our prayer become real; it is rightly directed; but it is also rightly guided by his Spirit, so our life is shaped by what is celebrated in the Church's worship and sustained in our prayer.

These convictions lie on every page of this book. Dr Glen O'Brien, like myself, has been shaped by the witness of the Wesley brothers and the Methodist movement. John Wesley's understanding of 'social holiness' is a balanced, practical theology, but his evangelism and his deep commitment to heal the ills of his society were rooted in reading the Scriptures, celebrating the sacraments, prayer, praise (not least his and his brother's hymns) and 'Christian conference'. From his daily prayer at 5 a.m. sprang his energy and his vision. He was a practical liturgist as well, and knew he had to make provision for 'right prayer' among his people, new to the faith or striving onwards, across the whole changing parish of his world.

Dr O'Brien makes these connections. As he lays out the evolving history of worship practice in the Christian Church, from the earliest days, through the special insights of the Reformation and the Wesleyan holiness movement, he also lays the rich fare of that Church's experience in worship before his readers: the wealth of cultures, of music and art and symbol, reminding us that human beings are body and spirit, persons and communities. What is unfamiliar by our ability to throw babies out with bathwater, he examines carefully before urging us to try things both old and new. He writes of worship as evangelical in all senses of the word. His ecumenical spirit is one which unites in spirit and truth. If, to some, he seems 'high church', it is because he is also 'high mission', and wants to encourage worship practice which is alive with the Gospel for today's multi-media and multi-choice society – while utterly faithful to the truth once received. Let those who read hear what the Spirit is saying to the churches!

Robert Gribben
Reformation Day 2012

Introduction

This book began as lectures for the unit *The Theology and Practice of Worship* taught over several years at Kingsley College, Melbourne. These were later developed into the Australian College of Ministry (ACOM) course *Worship Ministry*, in the Certificate IV in Christian Ministry. I am grateful to Kingsley College and ACOM for permission to reproduce this material in its present form. The material was also drawn upon by the North Thames Ministerial Training Course, ordination training provider for London and Chelmsford Dioceses of the Church of England and for Methodist candidates from London North of the Thames and Essex, UK. It is now hoped that this most recent form of the material may serve as an introductory liturgy text, for both vocational and degree level studies.

I am not a liturgist by profession, though both my formal theological education and pastoral practice have had a significant focus on liturgical and sacramental life and practice. In my second year at Asbury Theological Seminary I served as Sub-Prior of the Asbury Chapter of the Order of Saint Luke, a sacramental and liturgical order within the United Methodist Church, open to members of other denominations. Our primary activity was the offering of an early morning Eucharist, and I still remember with great fondness the crisp Kentucky mornings when we walked to the small "basement chapel" of the Beeson Centre to break bread together and celebrate Christ's presence among us. When given opportunities to choose a topic for a research paper I almost invariably chose to write on a sacramental or liturgical theme. Upon graduation I was pleased to receive the Hoyt L. Hickman Award for Excellence in Sacramental and Liturgical Scholarship and Practice. The chalice and paten gifted to me at that time are still in use in the congregation I served as pastor for eleven and half years upon my return to Australia. I mention these things not to draw attention to myself but so that the reader may be reassured that though I do not have formal qualifications in liturgical studies, worship is an area of Christian thought and practice that I have been closely involved with over many years.

The book has a simple design. It begins with an attempt to define Christian worship, considers worship in the Scriptures, and gives an historical overview of worship in the Church in five further chapters. The place of music, symbols, sacraments and the church year are all considered. This biblical, theological and historical grounding is important before moving on to more practical matters. In fact the inclusion of only a single chapter with a completely "practical" focus is quite deliberate. It arises out of the twin conviction that the best practice always arises out of the best theory, and that practical skills are mostly gained "on the job" in any case. This is not a "How to…" book, though it does suggest how we ought to think about worship and does make some practical suggestions.

The book is not addressed to a scholarly readership but to the interested beginner and the undergraduate student. It is best used to supplement a classroom setting where students can put the ideas they are learning into practice and receive helpful critique and encouragement from peers and from qualified instructors. Reflection questions at the end of each chapter may be used for small group discussion, personal journaling, or as a writing portfolio assessment task. Suggestions for further reading are provided at the end of each chapter for students who wish to go further.

ACKNOWLEDGMENTS

I am grateful to the many students who have taken my worship classes and contributed greatly to my own understanding of the field, and to the congregation at Spring Street Wesleyan Methodist Church, Prahran who sometimes wondered why I insisted on doing certain things that seemed to them as odd or not to their taste. I remain convinced that good liturgy contributes to good discipleship and that the more haphazard we are in our approach to worship the more haphazard will our Christian lives be as a result.

During my two years at Asbury Theological Seminary, I benefited greatly from the teaching of Professor Donald Boyd, to whom this book is dedicated. As an ordained elder in the Wesleyan Church with a deep love for the historic liturgy, Professor Boyd often felt himself to be fighting a losing battle trying to help his Wesleyan colleagues hold fast to their Methodist liturgical and sacramental heritage as well as gain a deeper appreciation for the worship of the whole Church. I find I have walked in his footsteps in this respect though my steps eventually took me out of the Wesleyan Methodist Church and into the Uniting Church.

Professor Gerard Moore, Lecturer in Worship and Practical Theology at Charles Sturt University, and formerly Head of Research at the Sydney College of Divinity, kindly looked over the material and gave me invaluable advice that filled in considerable gaps in my own knowledge. I thank Gerard for his help and for his suggestion that the material might make a good text book for an introductory liturgy unit.

Finally I wish to thank the Reverend Professor Emeritus Robert W. Gribben, retired Professor of Christian Worship at the Uniting Church Centre for Theology and Ministry in Parkville, Victoria and formerly minister of Wesley Uniting Church in Lonsdale Street, Melbourne. An erudite scholar, ecumenist, and mentor, he kindly agreed to read the manuscript and offered numerous helpful suggestions and corrections, and has contributed an insightful Preface. The feedback received from Professors Moore and Gribben has vastly improved this book, and I am in their debt.

CHAPTER ONE

What is Worship?

Christians form a worshipping community so learning how to worship is an important part of learning to be Christian. Of course, there is a sense in which worship is a universal human instinct and people of other religions worship even though they are not Christians. Yet there is something distinctive about Christian worship that arises out of a particular story – the story of God's saving work in Jesus Christ. It might be thought that since worship is instinctive there is little to be gained from writing a book about the technicalities of it all. It is true that worship is more like poetry than grammar. As important as it is to know the difference between a verb and a noun, how not to split infinitives, and how not to confuse subject and object, such rules of grammar are not important for their own sake; they exist so that poetry and novels and plays might be written and enjoyed. In the same way, there is a technical grammar of theology that informs and under girds our worship, but worship itself is something deeply intuitive and experiential.

Worship may be understood simply as the enjoyment of God. The origin of the English word "worship" is the old English "worth-ship," meaning to attribute worth to a person or thing. The seventeenth century *Westminster Larger Catechism* begins with the statement that "the chief end" [purpose] of humanity is "to glorify God and to enjoy Him forever."[1] Yet Christian worship is even more than this. In trying to define worship one might come up with definitions such as, "praising God," or "honouring God with our lives." These are good answers but they could equally be applied to the worship that takes place in other, non-Christian, religions. The distinctive thing about Christian worship is that it has the Triune God (Father, Son, and Holy Spirit) revealed in the person of Jesus Christ at the centre of it. The United Methodist minister Fred Craddock defines worship as "an assembly of believers [gathering]… to narrate in word, act, and song the community's memories and hopes, glorifying the God who redeems, enables, and sanctifies."[2] We might make a slight addition to this excellent definition – "an assembly of *Christian* believers," just to make sure!

Though all Christians worship, not all worship is good worship. There is worship that is pleasing to God, and then there is just doing our own thing.

---

1   *Westminster Larger Catechism* (1647), question 1.
2   Fred B. Craddock, *Preaching* (Nashville: Abingdon, 1985), 41.

There is an important concern for practical relevance in the church today and this is good, but we need to make sure that we don't conduct worship in ways that are seen to be "hip" or "trendy" without first ensuring that they are also theologically well grounded. There is a lot of pragmatism in the church today, which asks "does it work?" or "is it relevant?" without first asking "is it right?" Some worship services have the look and feel of entertainment rather than worship and the focus seems not to be on God but on the congregation (often thought of more as an "audience") and its assets and preferences. Behind every act of worship there are theological ideas. It's just that those ideas may not be well thought through; they may be imbalanced, immature, or just plain wrong.

Worship has sometimes been minimised to a reverent contemplation of the wonder of God as the divine mystery. At the other end of the spectrum, it has sometimes been seen as a method of interesting people in Christianity in an engaging and media-savvy way. Of course, there is certainly nothing wrong with the sheer experience of contemplating God's beauty, nor is there anything wrong with entertainment. But the focus of the Christian gathering, though it may include these things, is elsewhere. It has a narrative (*story*) element. On the first day of the week, Christians gather to retell their story of deliverance in continuity with the Israelite's exodus from Egypt.[3] As the Passover in Judaism is a family meal recounting deliverance from Egypt, so worship is a family gathering recounting the saving deliverance that God, in Christ, has wrought in us. We recount and celebrate the coming of the Lord Jesus Christ, his life, death, resurrection, and ascension. This is the theological basis of our worship. What we do in worship, the acts we perform are called the "liturgy" from the Greek word indicating the "work" that God's people do. When some people hear the word "liturgy" or "liturgical" they think of a very formal style of worship with many written prayers and responses and perhaps with a degree of formal ceremony attached. Actually in the study of worship the word "liturgy" refers to all acts of worship, whether formal or informal. There is a wide range of "sacred behaviours" the Church has developed in response to the mighty acts of God in Jesus Christ. Pentecostals who raise their hands, dance, and sing fast-paced songs to rock music arrangements have a liturgy just as do Orthodox Christians with their robed and bearded clergy, their incense, and their icons.[4] The style is different but both are "liturgies" and both tell (or should tell) the same story.

---

3   There are of course a few exceptions to worship on the first day of the week. Seventh-Day Adventists, Seventh-Day Baptists and Messianic Jews continue to worship on the seventh day.

4   The word "Orthodox" when the first letter is upper case refers to the Eastern Orthodox churches. When the word begins in lower case, except at the start of a sentence, it

Behind the current "worship wars" in the Church is the question of style. Do we have hymns or choruses or both? Should we be contemporary, traditional, or blended, high church, low church, or broad church? These sorts of questions are very much secondary to the real nature of worship. Whatever *style* is chosen, we are still left with the need to identify those unchanging constant elements that make up truly Christian worship. What are some of the basic principles that underlie the Church's worship, whatever particular style is adopted?

Worship is a Human Response to God's Own Self-Revelation

Worship only ever takes place as the result of God having revealed Godself to us. We love God only because God first loved us. The initiative is always with God. Jean-Pierre de Caussade warned against human-centred worship. "We ourselves must not try to produce spiritual pleasures and experiences, nor try to intensify those we may have. Such natural efforts are in direct opposition and quite contrary to the inspirations of the Holy Spirit. It is the bridegroom's voice which should awaken the soul."[5]

Andrew Blackwood, in *The Fine Art of Public Worship* long ago defined worship as humanity's response to God's self revelation, and stated that this response includes:

1. A feeling of awe and wonder in the Presence of the Holy God.
2. Confession of sins, personal and social [corporate].
3. The experience of God's cleansing and redeeming grace.
4. Dedication of the heart and life to God for service in the world.[6]

This last point (4) is important because our worship has profound social and political implications. There is a story, though it may well be apocryphal, about General William Booth, the founder of the Salvation Army, who was once offered a free telegraph message to be sent to every Salvation Army officer in the world, if he would limit the message to a single word. As the story goes, he thought for a while and then came up with the word he needed. It was the word "others." Unless the church's worship reaches out to connect with others it is not really having its full impact.

---

should be read as "holding to classical Christian doctrine as expressed in the Trinitarian faith of the Apostles' and Nicene Creeds."

5   Jean-Pierre de Caussade, *Abandonment to Divine Providence* (St. Louis: B. Herder, 1921), 77.

6   Andrew Blackwood, *The Fine Art of Public Worship* (Nashville: Abingdon Press, 1969), 14.

Blackwood's older definition, as good as it is, lacks the very important addition of reading, hearing and responding to God's Word, which are essential aspects of Christian worship. Indeed without hearing God speak the other elements of his list would be impossible. Isaiah 6:1-8 provides something of a biblical model of worship, with its call and response pattern. God initiates and Isaiah responds, leading to further self-revelation from God, and the harnessing of Isaiah's will in obedient service. Worship, then, is an encounter between God and people. The history of worship has been the history of God's self revelation. On God's side it is a gift of grace. On our side it calls for a response of thanksgiving and obedience. Abraham was not a "seeker" out in the desert searching for God or for "truth." He was a desert wanderer with a background in pagan idolatry, who, quite unexpectedly came face to face with the living God in the wilderness (Genesis 12:1-9). When God gave instructions to Moses about the Tabernacle (Exodus 25:1-9) and then later to Solomon about the Temple (1 Chronicles 28:11-19), he insisted that they be built strictly according to the pattern he established, right down to the precise measurements and the decorative details. It is God, rather than we, who sets the boundaries of worship. The important twentieth century theologian Karl Barth criticized the European liberal theology of his own day because it started with the human religious experience and built its theology from there. When they speak of God, Barth claimed, they are really only speaking of humanity in a very loud voice![7] If our worship is to avoid this error, we must worship from the starting point of God's own revelation in Christ.

Worship is Christ-Centred

Martin Luther used to say that the Bible was a harp upon which was played over and over again the same little song – Jesus Christ given for us. Worship is the Church's song about Jesus. Worship that centres only on God simply as the Supreme Being would not be Christian worship. Worship that centred only on the Holy Spirit would not be Christian worship, but could become fanaticism. There is a *particularity* about Christian worship – its focus is not on "the divine" in some vague way, but on a *particular* God with a *particular* history in the world – the God of Abraham, Isaac, and Jacob, the God who brought the Israelites through the Red Sea on dry ground, the God and Father of our Lord Jesus Christ, the God who raised Jesus from the dead.

My son attended a denominational school and some of the parents were concerned that while there were religion classes and chapels nothing very distinctively Christian was ever said in them. I noted as I attended assemblies

7   Karl Barth, *The Word of God and the Word of Man*, trans. *Douglas Horton* (Gloucester, MA: Peter Smith, 1978), 196.

and speech nights that this church-owned and operated high school seemed very careful never to mention the name of Jesus or to refer in any way to any distinctively Christian truth claims. In response to the concerns of parents that this didn't seem right for a Christian school, the Principal replied, "We are not a Christian school; we are a church school." Apparently in his mind it was possible to be a church organization without necessarily also being Christian! This is what can happen when we lose our particular way of speaking. As Bishop William Willimon has said, "Christians speak funny."[8] We have a distinct language because we have a unique story to tell. We should not apologise for this but embrace it because when we give up speaking our own language, we lose our story. And our story is focused on Jesus Christ as the one who reveals God to us.

Worship should focus on Jesus Christ, his incarnation, his life, his death, his resurrection, his ascension, his presence in heaven, his presence in our midst, and his coming again. Of course, this is not to deny that Christian worship is Trinitarian (see below), but we know God in Trinity only through God the Son. Jesus said to Philip, "Whoever has seen me has seen the Father" (John 14:9). We know the Father because he sent his Son. The Holy Spirit comes to speak, not of himself, but of Christ (John 16:5-16). We are reconciled to God only through Christ. It is Christ who baptises with the Holy Spirit (Matthew 3:11). We are the Body of Christ (Romans 12:5). In short, the Christian Church is found wherever the risen Christ is present in the midst of the worshipping community.

Worship is Trinitarian

Brian Edgar states in no uncertain terms that Christian belief in the Trinity is "fundamentally simple, thoroughly practical, theologically central and totally biblical."

> It is not, as sometimes suggested, an abstract or philosophical construction with an unusual perspective on mathematics which makes three equal to one! It is not a doctrine which is incomprehensible in presentation, irrelevant in practice, unnecessary theologically or unbiblical in form. It is in fact the distinctive Christian doctrine and essential for Christian life and discipleship.[9]

Nineteenth century liberal theology had a tendency to sideline the doctrine of the Trinity as something of little significance and of dubious value. Beginning with the work of Karl Barth in the mind-twentieth century, however, the importance of the Trinity took centre stage in theological reflection until

---

8   William Willimon, *Peculiar Speech: Preaching to the Baptised* (Grand Rapids, MI: Eerdmans, 1992).

9   Brian Edgar, *The Message of the Trinity* (Leicester: Inter-Varsity Press, 2004), 20.

today there is a broad consensus that the whole project of theology, as well as the entire foundation of the Christian life, is grounded in the nature of God as Triune. According to Michael Jinkins, "The meaning and the shaping of our life together as a community of persons is grounded in the inner life of God, the Trinity, and has been revealed to us in the life, death and resurrection of Jesus Christ."[10]

I think it's fair to say that these gains in theology have not always found their way into our worship practices. A famous wartime propaganda campaign declared "loose lips sink ships" and there is a lot of loose speaking in our worship that threatens to capsize a proper Trinitarian emphasis. For example, one hears a lot of what theologians have called "confounding of the Persons." "Dear Father, we thank you Lord Jesus that you died on the cross for us..." Now, of course, the Father did not die on the cross, but the Son. Sometimes you will hear a prayer like the following: "We thank you Father Lord that Lord Jesus you came Father God and helped us Lord to see, Jesus, that we are never alone Father..." and so on. As well as confounding the persons, this prayer borders on blasphemy because in using words like "Father" and "Lord" as a substitute for "um or "ah," as the person collects his or her thoughts, the speaker uses the Lord's name "in vain" (i.e. in an "empty" or mindless way). My advice here would be to slow down, speak more slowly, and think about what is being said. Of course God looks at the heart and when Christians pray in a theologically loose way or in a way not quite "proper" or not fully Trinitarian this does not mean that those prayers go unheeded. God is patient with us, of course, but congregational leaders have the responsibility of modelling best practice.

Almost invariably, prayer in the New Testament is offered to God the Father, in the name of Jesus, and through the Holy Spirit. The exceptions are when Stephen was being stoned to death and he looked up to heaven, saw Jesus and prayed, "Lord Jesus, receive my spirit" (Acts 7:59) and the prayer near the end of Revelation, "Amen. Come Lord Jesus!" (Rev. 22:20). I am not aware of any prayer in the New Testament made directly to the Holy Spirit. This does not mean that prayer directly to Jesus or the Spirit is wrong. However, the general biblical pattern seems to be a Trinitarian one in which the Father is addressed on the basis of what Christ has done and with the authority that lies behind his name, and (since we don't know how to pray as we ought) the Spirit helps us in our weakness by interceding within us, empowering and enabling our speech (Rom 8:26-27).

---

10   Michael Jinkins, *Invitation to Theology* (Downers Grove: Inter-Varsity Press, 2001), 19.

Some people say that Pentecostals focus too much on the Spirit in their worship but the tendency among Christians of all persuasions is to confess belief in the Trinity but to be functionally Unitarian (there is one God and his name is "Jesus") or "binitarian" ("God and Jesus" with no Holy Spirit to be seen). It is a pity that the ancient *Gloria Patri* ("Glory be to the Father, and to the Son, and to the Holy Spirit; as it was in the beginning, is now and shall be forever, world without end. Amen") is not used as much as it used to be, because it enshrined a Trinitarian doxology in every service.

The use of Trinitarian benedictions help us maintain a focus on God as Triune as do Trinitarian hymns and songs. However, Reginald Heber's *Holy, Holy, Holy* (as great as it is) is not the only Trinitarian hymn available. Consider the final verse of *Now Thank We All Our God*.

> All praise and thanks to God the Father now be given; The Son and Holy Ghost, supreme in highest Heaven; The one eternal God, whom earth and Heaven adore; For thus it was, is now, and shall be evermore.[11]

This can be separated from the rest of the hymn as a stand alone Trinitarian doxology that could be sung, for example, as a response to the Psalm or other Bible reading. Just because a song has "Father, Son, and Holy Spirit" in the lyrics does not mean, however, that it is Trinitarian. Some songs are quite theologically incoherent (that is, they don't "co-here" or "hold together"). For example, there is a popular worship song that alters the order of the names in the Trinitarian formula, placing "Son" after "Spirit" in order that "Son" may rhyme with the word "one" in the previous line. The placement of the words "Father, Son and Holy Spirit" is not just traditional but deeply theological in its ordering. The Father *begets* the Son, the Spirit *proceeds from* the Father (or from the Father and the Son if one accepts the western form of the Nicene Creed). Making a fuss over the ordering of words may seem like liturgical fundamentalism to some but the way we address God in worship is an important matter that deserves serious reflection.

Often among very large groups of worshippers, we see each person wrapped in his or her own personal bubble of worshipful intimacy, eyes closed, communing with Jesus, their "personal Saviour." In such settings it is difficult to see how any one person is present to any other person. Transcended beyond others to a private space shared only between God and themselves, they do not face each other, or engage in any way with their fellow worshippers. If God, as Trinity, is a Being whose very existence is a reciprocal, relational one, our worship should reflect that reciprocity by being more communal than personal and ecstatic. This is not in any way to question the validity of

---

11   *Together in Song* (Australian Hymn Book II) no. 106.

mystical experience as a deeply personal mode of spirituality. But Christian liturgy is a public act whereby the believing community engages in joint activity. We greet one another with a sign of peace. We gather together at the Lord's Table. Responsive readings of Scripture and the recitation together of prayers and confessions of faith are participatory actions performed together in a reciprocal exchange. Ecstatic experiences of God have their place but the true "ex-stasis" is to be "outside of" oneself in order to be *for* the other.

Worship is the Work of the Church

While it is possible to worship alone, and we certainly should do that, Christian worship is designed to be a community act; it's a "churchy" thing, a corporate activity of the whole family of God. Most of our confusion over worship stems from our confusion over the nature of the Church. Why do we "go to" church? To hear a great sermon, enjoy good music, make new friends, or consume tea and biscuits? We may do all of those things in church and enjoy them, but are these the reasons we go? We could do any of these things at any number of other civic or social clubs or societies. We *go* to church to *be* the church, that is, to worship God as a community in Jesus Christ, and through the Holy Spirit.

The Church exists for the purpose of worship. Of course, this is not confined to what takes place in gathered services of worship, since all of life is in one sense an act of worship (Romans 12:1). At the same time, activities such as evangelism, community engagement and social justice are activities that are extensions of the liturgy. They are the overflow of the liturgy, and are in fact themselves an expression of worship beyond the gathered meeting time. We often hear it said today that the Church is the only organisation that exists not primarily for the benefit of its members, but for those on the outside. This sounds right at first, but on closer examination, is not quite the truth. The Church exists neither for its own benefit, nor for the benefit of the unevangelised, at least not primarily. It exists for the glory of God. John Wesley's oft-quoted saying, "You have nothing to do but save souls; therefore spend and be spent in this work," is understood wrongly if taken to mean that the Church is nothing more than one great big evangelism machine.[12] Wesley was not addressing the Church as such at all, but his chosen band of itinerant evangelists, all (or most) of whom were already members of the Church of England and expected to engage, along with other Methodists, in the Church's weekly liturgy. To take advice addressed to a society of evangelists and make of it the reason for the Church's whole existence, runs the danger of making

---

12   John Wesley, 'Twelve Rules of a Helper,' *Minutes of Several Conversations* (1789) in *Works* (Jackson edition) VIII:310.

worship merely a means to an end. If evangelism and social engagement do not spring from a worshipping lifestyle, they may become no more than a type of works-righteousness by which we try to earn brownie points with God or workaholism driven by our own need for significance.

The Shape of Christian Worship

There are three elements to any worship service - Content, Structure and Style. Of these, *Content* is primary. "For worship to be biblical and Christian, the story of God's redemption and salvation must be its content. Otherwise it ceases to be Christian worship. For it is the content of worship – the Gospel – that makes worship uniquely and distinctly Christian."[13] There is no biblically mandated structure for worship. There are no orders of service provided in the Scriptures, and no convenient blueprints for worship planners to go by. In the absence of such material, our next port of call is the practice of the Church from its beginning. When we examine the history as well as the current practice of worship, we find four basic actions reoccurring.

- Assembling the people (Gathering)
- Scripture reading and preaching (The Service of the Word)
- Response to the Word (Eucharist)[14]
- Sending the people forth (Dismissal)

Participation in liturgical renewal in all of the mainline churches has brought about a remarkable consensus on this four-fold action as being the basic shape of the liturgy.[15] Style is then the atmosphere in which the preceding four acts or "movements" are played out. Styles may vary but content must not. It may be contemporary, traditional, highly liturgical, quite informal, or any combination of them all. Each congregation constructs its own style but cannot dispense with the nature of worship as a proclamation of the Gospel. Let's take a quick look at each of these four movements in turn.

---

13   Robert Webber, *Worship Old and New* (Grand Rapids: Zondervan, 1995), 150.

14   In services where the Eucharist is not celebrated, this movement may include other acts of thanksgiving, such as prayers, offerings, and acts of Christian initiation. However, an argument could be made that such substitutions fall short of the fullness intended. There is in the Last Supper a mandate given by Christ - "Do this in remembrance of me." This act of *anamnesis* (remembrance) cannot easily be set aside. It is widely recognised by liturgists that a proper Christian worship service should be a full service of Word *and* Table.

15   Stephen Burns, *Worship and Ministry: Shaped towards God* (Melbourne: Mosaic Press, 2012), 19-22.

A. Gathering

This is no mere human act because the church is called together (*ekklesia*) by God with Jesus as the new focus of our assembling, replacing the old sacrificial system with a "new and living way." There are various ways that the church might gather together.

- Silence
- Procession
- Greeting
- Call to Worship (addressed to the people)
- Invocation (addressed to God)
- Musical Preface
- Hymn or Song

B. The Service of the Word

After gathering in response to God's call, we hear what God has to say to us by giving attention to the Scriptures. The public reading of Scripture is at least as old as Moses delivering the Ten Commandments on Mt. Sinai. It was central to the regathering of the Jews under Ezra and Nehemiah. The reading of Scripture should not be seen as merely preliminary to the sermon but as a time when God speaks. Priority has historically been given to the Gospels and this has been expressed liturgically by standing for the reading of the Gospels. It is always appropriate for the people to respond to the reading of the Scriptures. If "This is the Word of the Lord" followed by "Thanks be to God!" seems too formal, there should at least be a spoken, "Amen!" It is quite inappropriate to read the Bible and then just abruptly end with no affirmation that what has just been heard is a form of divine speech. It is especially ironic that Evangelicals who affirm a high view of the inspiration and authority of Scripture should sometimes approach the reading of the Bible in a casual and haphazard way. Evangelicals sometimes criticise the (so-called) liturgical churches, and yet in a typical Roman Catholic, Anglican or Orthodox service, one will hear a Psalm, an Old Testament[16] reading, an Epistle reading and a Gospel reading, whereas often the only reading in an Evangelical church will be the sermon text (and sometimes not even that!). After we have heard the Scriptures read, we hear them expounded in proclamation. Preaching should

---

16   The use of the term "Old Testament" is not meant to convey disrespect to people of Jewish faith for whom the Hebrew Scripture are certainly not "old" in the sense of "outdated." Alternatives such as "First Testament" and "Hebrew Scriptures" were considered, but the traditional term was chosen simply because of its wider currency.

involve both *kerygma* (that is, it should announce or proclaim the good news) as well as *didache* (that is, it should teach).

C. Thanksgiving

After hearing God speak through the Scriptures, the people give thanks for, and respond to, what they have heard. This may include such elements as

- Prayers of thanksgiving and intercession.
- The offering (better here than before the sermon, because it comes as a response to God's word to us).
- Acts of dedication and commitment – baptism, confirmation, altar call, reception into church membership.
- The Lord's Supper ("Eucharist" means "thanksgiving" and this is the most appropriate way for the church to give thanks).[17]
- The Actions of the Communion Service
    - Invitation (inviting those who love God and seek to love God more to partake of the meal).
    - Prayer of Great Thanksgiving (recalling the mighty saving acts of God in creating and redeeming the world).
    - The Words of Institution (Recalling Jesus' institution of the Supper - "On the night that he was betrayed Jesus took bread…and said "This is my body…This is my blood.")
    - The Supper Itself
        - Taking (the elements of bread and wine).
        - Blessing (asking God's Spirit to bless these elements and all those who partake of them).
        - Breaking (recalling Jesus' actions at the Last Supper).
        - Giving (distributing the elements to the faithful).

---

17   For an excellent theological and practical commentary on one particular denomination's Eucharistic Prayers see Robert Gribben, *Uniting in Thanksgiving: The Great Prayers of Thanksgiving of the Uniting Church in Australia* (Melbourne: Uniting Academic Press, 2008).

Prayers of intercession have historically been an important part of the church's liturgy but a disturbing trend sees this undergoing a change. Professor David Bebbington, a leading historian of British evangelicalism from the University of Stirling is also a keen observer and commentator on worship practices. At a lecture series at Ridley College in 2006, Bebbington was asked what he believed had been the major change in worship in the United Kingdom over the last forty years. His reply was disturbing. It was Bebbington's observation that intercessory prayer - prayer for others beyond the congregation - had all but disappeared in Evangelical and Charismatic churches. There is plenty of prayer for those present in the church. Many people receive prayer at the altar for all kinds of personal, physical, emotional, and spiritual problems, but prayer is rarely offered for anyone not present. This alarming trend suggests that the Church may be losing an understanding of its 'priestly' role. We are called to intercede for the world, for political leaders, for church leaders, for the sick, for the hungry, for the homeless, for those who struggle with mental illness, for those trapped in substance abuse, and for all those who cannot or will not pray for themselves.

D. Dismissal

Here in this final movement we "go forth to love and serve the Lord." Worship continues now, in the world we are called to serve. We go out into our mission field. Worship leaders often struggle with finding an appropriate time for the church notices that does not disrupt the flow of worship. Giving such announcements during the Dismissal seems appropriate as they relate to the week's coming activities beyond the liturgy itself. Worship is a vision of the new creation – the way the world ought to be. We now go out to implement that vision. In the benediction and blessing – just as God calls us to worship, God now speaks words of blessing in dismissing us. There is a difference between a closing prayer and a benediction that is often not observed. A benediction (literally "good words") is spoken by the leader to the people on behalf of God. It should, therefore, be spoken with eyes open to the congregation and hands held up in blessing. The congregation should not bow their heads and close their eyes but look up to receive the blessing, responding with a hearty "Amen." A closing prayer, on the other hand, is addressed to God, rather than to the congregation, and so bowed heads and closed eyes are appropriate. A good way to train people in this regard is to pray a closing prayer ending with an "Amen," at which point people will open their eyes and look up. You may then welcome them to "receive this benediction" and with hands extended in blessing, announce the "good words" of dismissal to them.

Toward a Definition of Christian Worship

Perhaps we may begin now to move toward an adequate definition of worship: Christian worship is human response to the Triune God's self-revelation, expressed in celebration of, and thanksgiving for, God's saving activity in Jesus Christ. Following on from this definition, there is the important matter of the order, style, and content of worship. However, unless we have this kind of foundation, our worship, though orderly in its own way, and even artistically pleasing, and culturally accessible, will nonetheless be something less than truly Christian.

Some Questions

1. Has your reading of this chapter changed or added to the ways you may have previously understood worship? If so, in what way?

2. Describe what can happen in the church's worship when we focus on what is *relevant* more than on what is *right*. What is the role of relevance in Christian worship?

3. What is the worship "style" of your own local church? Does it typically follow the movements of "Gathering, Hearing the Word, Thanking, and Dismissal" or some other pattern? If not, in what ways does it diverge from this pattern?

4. What are the particular "pressure points" in your own congregation about worship? What seems to push people's buttons? Or are you blessed with a relatively conflict-free environment when it comes to worship?

5. What are some ways the church is pressured to lose its own unique speech and story and what is the impact of this on our worship?

6. Consider the definition at which we arrived. "Christian worship is human response to the Triune God's self-revelation, expressed in celebration of, and thanksgiving for, God's saving activity in Jesus Christ." How might you improve upon this definition?

Further Reading:

Stephen Burns, *Worship and Ministry: Shaped towards God*. Melbourne: Mosaic Press, 2012

Burns, Stephen and Anita Monro, eds. *Christian Worship in Australia: Inculturating the Liturgical Tradition*. Sydney: St. Paul's 2009.

Byars, Ronald P. *The Future of Protestant Worship: Beyond the Worship Wars*. Louisville/London: Westminster John Knox Press, 2002.

Dawn, Marva. *Reaching Out Without Dumbing Down: A Theology of Worship for This Urgent Time*. Grand Rapids: Eerdmans, 1995.

___. *A Royal "Waste" of Time: The Splendor of Worshiping God and Being Church for the World*. Grand Rapids: Eerdmans, 1999.

Wainwright, Geoffrey. *Doxology: The Praise of God in Worship, Doctrine, and Life - A Systematic Theology*. New York: Oxford University Press, 1980.

Robert Webber, *Worship Old and New*. rev. ed. Grand Rapids: Zondervan, 1995.

White, James F. *Introduction to Christian Worship*. 3rd Edition. Nashville: Abingdon Press, 2001.

CHAPTER TWO

Worship in the Old Testament

The Role of Liturgy in the Formation of Scripture

While it often insisted that liturgy must be built on a biblical foundation, what is often overlooked is that the Bible itself is in one sense built on a liturgical foundation. The Church reflects on what it has experienced of God's grace, and takes action in the world arising out of that experience.[1] One of the actions it takes is to record its experience in Scripture. So even though it is proper to say that Scripture is normative for worship, at the same time, worship itself contributed in a very significant way to the formation of Scripture. Many passages in the Old Testament arise out of and have their origins in the liturgical patterns of the ancient Israelites. Similarly the Gospels and letters of the New Testament are derived from the Church's gathered life experiences and often address liturgical concerns.

Worship as a Gift of God's Grace

The Old Testament clearly takes the view that it is God who establishes the forms in which God is to be worshipped. In reading about worship you will probably come across the term "cult." It's important not to mistake this to mean a religious group with unorthodox ideas, as we usually use the term. The term "cult" in the study of religion means the formal and ritual aspects by which a community expresses its worship. In the Hebrew Bible, God himself establishes the "cult" of Israel. The many symbols and rituals of Old Testament worship instructed the Israelites in God's nature and ways. These symbolic actions were not "dead rites," but gifts of God's grace to his ancient people. Symbols instruct us in moving from outer forms to inner realities helping worshippers to draw near to God. We should not think in terms of "those poor Israelites weighed down with all those animal sacrifices, rituals and laws." We should remember instead that the Law was a gift of grace, and that the liturgies of the priestly offerings, of the Tabernacle, and of the Temple, were all expressions of God's covenant love.

Worship as Festival

Worship in the Old Testament is narrated as the establishment of sacred space, sacred time and sacred acts. Sacred spaces from the simple stone altars

---

1   Louis-Marie Chauvet, *Symbole et Sacrement* (Paris: Editions du Cerf), 1990, published in English as *Symbol and Sacrament: A Sacramental Reinterpretation of Christian Experience*, trans. Patrick Madigan (Collegeville, MN, 1995), 179.

of the patriarchs to the ornate magnificence of Solomon's temple were places of encounter with God. Sacred time was marked by festivals, often tied in with seasons and harvests such as Pentecost (Exodus 23:16; Numbers 28:26-31; Deut. 16:9-12), or memorials of God's saving power, such as the Passover (Leviticus 23:5; Exodus 23:14-15; Joshua 5:10-12), and the Festival of Booths or Tabernacles (Leviticus 23:39-43; Exodus 23:16; Deuteronomy 16:13). These remind us that Old Testament religion was not a gloomy affair, concerned exclusively with sin, atonement, and repentance, though these matters were taken with the utmost seriousness. It was, and the Jewish religion remains, a festival of celebration over the goodness of God. Of course the Sabbath is the most significant of all the ways the Jewish people mark time. The seventh day serves as a sign of the covenant between God and Israel and is a weekly reminder of the obligations upon God's people to be loyal to that covenant. The sacred acts of circumcision, priestly washings, and dietary laws of the Old Testament were all ways in which God's people were set apart from the surrounding nations as belonging exclusively to Yahweh.[2]

Worship as Engaging with God

According to David Peterson, "from a biblical point of view, the worship of the living and true God is essentially an engagement with him on the terms that he proposes and in the way that he alone makes possible."[3] Peterson's helpful study of the biblical theology of worship concludes that worship in Old Testament times was understood as essentially "honouring, serving, and respecting God." It is an attitude of homage or adoration to God as a great king. There was an intimacy between God and the worshiper but it wasn't the kind of relationship we think of when we use the word "intimacy" today. Not so much a feeling of special affection, intimacy with God was an expression of awe or of grateful submission to his rule over all of life. Worship was seen as service rendered to God - the acknowledgment of God's divine kingship in personal and national life. It involved reverence or fear of the Lord – the honouring of God by a total lifestyle.[4]

Worship and Music

All the way through this book we will take note of the role that music has played in worship. Before going on to discuss the use of music in the Old Testament, it is worth taking a little time to think about music in worship

---

2   "Yahweh" is the English equivalent of the "tetragammaton" -YHWH – the Hebrew word used to stand in the place of the Name of God. The Name was considered so holy that it could not be spoken or written.

3   David Peterson, *Engaging with God: A Biblical Theology of Worship* (Leicester: Apollos, 1992), 55.

4   Peterson, 70-74.

generally. As far as we know music has always been connected with the religious life of humanity. At first the use of music in worship seems to have been "ecstatic" and spontaneous in nature, rather than structured or notated. Only at a later stage did it develop form, with accompanying rules and patterns. We know that in ancient Egypt, small cymbals and more complex instruments such as harps of twelve or thirteen strings were used. The Greeks used music in their worship of the gods, and believed that music had a moral, spiritual, and emotional influence over humans. Plutarch, for example said, "The right moulding of ingenuous manners and civil conduct lies in a well-grounded musical education."[5] Music was listed, along with arithmetic and geometry, as one of the seven "liberal arts" of the ancient Greek world. It was considered not only something aesthetic (to do with art and taste), but something philosophical and "scientific." It was under Greek influence that notation and the ordering of a musical system first took place.

Though there are some Christian traditions that do not approve of instrumental music in worship and some, such as the Quakers, highly value receptive silence, these are exceptions that seem to prove the rule that worship and music go together. In Roman Catholic worship, music is used as an accompaniment to the liturgy. It is very closely related to the rite and is seen as an integral part of the worship being offered. In this sense it is in continuity with the ancient Hebrew understanding of the spiritual efficacy of music in the antiphonal chanting of the Psalms, as discussed later in this chapter. Mainline Protestants tend to use hymns and songs as an act of prayer. The opening hymn often ascribes praise to God; there is typically a hymn after the sermon as a form of response, and a closing hymn of dismissal. It is a commonplace that music, in particular hymn singing, formed an important part of the appeal of the early Methodists. Edward Miller, the organist at Doncaster parish church, Yorkshire complained about the Methodists' popularity. "It is well known that more people are drawn to the tabernacles of the Methodists by their attractive harmony, than by the doctrine of their preachers…Where the Methodists have drawn *one* person from our [Church of England] by their preaching, they have drawn *ten* by their music."[6] The worldwide growth of Pentecostalism throughout the twentieth century no doubt had much to do with the significant place music has had in the movement.

To return now to music in the Old Testament - though the Hebrews recognised the impact of music on the emotions, such as when David's playing lifted the depression of Saul (1 Samuel 16:23), their primary concern was to

---

5   Kenneth W. Osbeck, *The Ministry of Music* (Grand Rapids: Kregel, 1971), 17.
6   *Christian History* 31 (1991):17.

utilise music in the worship of Yahweh. "For the Hebrews, the arts obtained significance only as they could be used to adorn the courts of Jehovah or could be employed in the ascription of praise to Him."[7] According to A. S. Herbert, the connection between the sacrifices, and the musical chanting that accompanied it, did not perform a merely artistic function, but was thought to bring about real religious power. "They are not merely pious reflections, but effective words through which Israel's 'soul' was conveyed to God, and His energy in judgment and renewal was released into Israel's soul and through that into the world of nature and man."[8]

The first mention of music in the Bible is found in Genesis 4:21 where Jubal is said to have been the "ancestor of all those who play the lyre and pipe." There are about thirteen instruments mentioned in the Bible, which can be classified into stringed instruments, wind instruments, and percussion instruments. Stringed instruments include the *kinnor* (lyre) and the *nephel* a ten stringed *harp* (called a "psaltery" in the King James Version). Among the wind instruments were the *shophar* (ram's horn), *halil* (a double-reed, oboe-like instrument), *hazozerah* (a metal trumpet), and *ugabh* (a vertical flute). Percussion instruments included the *toph* (tambourine, or hand drum), *zelzelim* (cymbals), and *mena an im* (sistrum or rattle).[9]

The first reference to music explicitly in connection with worship is found in Exodus 15:1-2, 20-21 where Moses and Miriam offered thanksgiving to God for the deliverance from Egypt. We note that this was both instrumental and vocal music, and included both women and men. Virtually the same narrative found here is delivered again in several Psalms – for example Ps. 78:12-13, and 136:10-15. Other songs in the Old Testament include the song of Deborah and Barak (Judges 5:3), Hannah's song of thanksgiving (1 Samuel 2:1-10) and David's song of thanksgiving and deliverance from Saul (2 Samuel 22).

The words "music," "musicians," "musical instruments," "song," "singers," and "singing" appear in the Bible 575 times, in 44 of the 66 books. The whole of the Book of Psalms (150 chapters) is made up entirely of songs, originally used with musical settings. It's easy for us to forget this, when our use of the Psalms is often non-musical, with the exception, of course, of Scots (and Gaelic) Presbyterianism where the Psalms continue regularly to be sung. "The psalms were sung in regular sequence following the morning and evening sacrifices

---

7   Osbeck, 17.

8   A. S. Herbert, *Worship in Ancient Israel* (Richmond: John Knox Press, 1959), 26.

9   Drawn from Donald P. Hustad, *Jubilate II: Church Music in Worship and Renewal* (Carol Stream: Hope Publishing, 1993), 134. It should be recognised that there is not uniform agreement on the precise definition of the musical instruments mentioned in the Bible, and that the precise meaning of the Hebrew word 'Selah' is uncertain.

on specified days of the week and were accompanied by instruments which occasionally may have interrupted the singing with an interlude, possibly indicated by the word 'Selah.'"[10]

Two Worship Traditions

Erik Routley identifies two worship traditions in the Old Testament: one spontaneous and ecstatic, the other formal and professional.[11] An example of the first is given in 1 Samuel 10:5-6 where we read that the prophet Samuel is told that he will encounter a "band of prophets" at Gibeah-elohim, who will be playing harp, tambourine, flute, and lyre in "a prophetic frenzy. Then the spirit of the Lord will possess you, and you will be in a prophetic frenzy along with them and be turned into a different person." Much of the material we find in the prophetic books of the Bible is in poetic style, divided into verses or stanzas, indicating that they may have been originally chanted or sung. Music was often seen as accompanying a state of religious ecstasy or transport, under which the prophet exercised his gift. For example, on one occasion, Elisha called for a musician and then while the musician played, "the power of the Lord came on him" and he foretold the impending judgment of God (2 Kings 3:14-16a).

The music used in the worship of the tabernacle in the wilderness, its settlement under David, and later the Temple under Solomon is an example of Routley's second type – formal liturgical music. Here we see a very elaborate development of the musical life of Israel. David was himself a musician and a composer, and his influence on the Tabernacle worship is very clear. The Levites, an entire priestly tribe, were given the responsibility of providing musical training for the leadership of these services. Under David, the first large-scale choir and orchestra were organized for use in the Tabernacle worship.

The priest-musicians gave all their time to musical service. They were chosen on the basis of talent (1 Chronicles 15:22), and were provided with thorough training, including a five-year musical apprenticeship before admission to the band. Asaph, Heman, and Jeduthun seemed to be responsible for the Jewish choir as composers and conductors (2 Chronicles 5:12). Under Solomon the musical grandeur of the nation increased even more. 2 Chronicles 5:13-14 gives a description of the worship of the temple, including a large group of singers and instrumentalists clothed in white robes. The worship of this period appealed to all five senses, including visual symbols such as priestly vestments, and candles, smells such as incense and burning animal flesh, tastes such as the shared offerings, and of course, the auditory appeal of music. The Jewish

---

10   Hustad, 137.

11   Erik Routley, *Church Music and the Christian Faith* (Carol Stream: Agape, 1978), 6.

historian Josephus records that in the first temple "there were 20,000 trumpets and 200,000 robed singers and instrumentalists, arrayed in white linen gowns, taking part in the service."[12] Even if this is an overstatement, it at least refers to a considerably large group of musicians serving at that time.

After the return from captivity in Babylon, temple worship was restored in the Second Temple. (This was the temple that stood in Jesus' day, which is referred to in the New Testament, only the ruins of which were left after the destruction of Jerusalem by the Roman imperial army in 70 CE). Though this was not quite as magnificent as Solomon's temple, music still played a large part in the services offered there. The Jewish Talmud describes the psalm singing of the Second Temple. At a given sign from the cymbals, twelve Levites stood on the broad staircase leading from the congregation to the court of the priests and played on nine lyres, two harps and one cymbal. As this happened, the priests poured out the wine offering. Young Levitical boys added their voices to the treble part. The pauses, or divisions, or "selahs" of the Psalm were indicated by the blast of trumpets to the left and right of the cymbal players.

There was a very strong connection between the words of Holy Scripture and the music of the Old Testament liturgy. According to Hustad, "the words of ancient scripture were not to be spoken without melody; to do so was considered to be a minor sacrilege."[13] And so, the Scriptures were not simply read, but chanted. This chanting was accompanied by musical instruments, which provided embellishments of the vocal melody. Many Psalms are constructed in parallel patterns, giving rise to the suggestion that they were originally, sung *antiphonally*, that is divided into a "versicle" sung by the cantor (song leader) and a "response" sung by the choir. The music was mostly priestly and professional, rather than congregational, though the people would join in traditional responses such as "Amen," and "Alleluia."

What Did All Of This Sound Like?

The music sung and played in Old Testament worship would have sounded quite unlike anything we hear in our churches today. In fact it would in all likelihood sound quite foreign to our ears and culturally distant, to the point of being jarring. Some modern day Jewish cantors claim that the chants heard in the synagogues of today are substantially unchanged since biblical times, because of the strength of oral tradition that has passed them on. Some musicologists believe that Eastern Orthodox chants, especially those of the Ethiopian Church, have preserved much of the original music of the Old

12   Osbeck, 17.
13   Hustad, 134.

Testament since the early Christians were keen to preserve the Hebrew music that accompanied the text in synagogue usage.

Eric Werner points out that the consensus among the leading authorities is that the early Hebrew chants were based on four-note chords and melodic patterns, much like Gregorian chants with their narrow range, not exceeding a fourth or fifth.[14] The French musician and scholar Suzanne Haik Vantoura, believes that her research demonstrates that the notations above and below Jewish letters, usually understood as accent marks for chanting, are in fact a system of musical notation. Based on this she has transcribed and recorded several hours of music from the Bible.[15]

Drawn from Pagan Models?

The Old Testament scholar, Ronald Allen has argued that Israel's songs were adaptations of pagan tunes, taken from the musical heritage of Canaan and the broader Ancient Near East. He maintains that Israel did not just borrow the "secular" music of the surrounding pagan culture but the "sacred" music, used in the worship of the pagan deities.[16] An example of this is Psalm 29, which is thought by many biblical scholars to be based on an ancient Canaanite song.[17] Hustad depends on such evidence to maintain the position he takes that "sacred music forms are often based on earlier, unsanctified models."[18] This practice continues today as secular styles of music are often adopted by the church for use in worship.

Worship in the Synagogue

The most significant religious innovation among the Hebrews after the Babylonian exile, which has continued to this day, is the synagogue. This was developed to maintain a sense of religious identity in the Jewish *diaspora* (the spread of Jewish people throughout the known world) far from the temple and the homeland. Whether this development took place first during the Babylonian captivity, or later during the Second Temple period, in lands other than Israel, is a point of dispute among scholars. In either case, because the animal sacrifices could not be offered beyond the temple, the emphasis on verbal and musical worship was the offering of the "sacrifice of prayer and

---

14   Eric Werner, "Jewish Music," in *Grove's Dictionary*, Vol. IV (New York: St. Martin's Press, 1954), 623.

15   Suzanne Haik Vantoura, *The Music of the Bible Revealed*, translated by Dennis Weber (Berkeley: Bible Press, 1991), 364-5. For an example, based on Psalm 46:11, see Hustad, 136.

16   Roland Allen, "The Psalmist," in *Worship Leader*, I:3 (June-July 1992), 5.

17   Hans-Joachim Kraus, *Psalms 1-59: A Commentary*, translated by Hilton C. Oswald (Minneapolis: Augsburg, 1988), 346-7.

18   Hustad, 135.

praise." The pattern of synagogue worship, with its reading and teaching of scripture, prayers, and the singing of psalms and canticles, would come to form the basis of early Christian worship, with the distinctively Christian addition of the Eucharist. Synagogue music was probably led, as it is today, by a cantor - a soloist, probably trained in the Levitical temple service – and included congregational participation, such as responses. Synagogue worship was formal, rather than ecstatic, used a set lectionary of Scripture readings, and was based on the liturgical cycle of seasons – the annual cycle of fasts and festivals. Much of this was carried over into Christian worship in its earliest period.

Summary

So let's summarise what we have learned about worship in the Old Testament. The Israelites believed that it was God who determined the way we should worship by revealing to Moses the precise liturgy of the offerings and all that should take place in the Tent of Meeting. We worship God only because God has first been revealed to us. The worship of the Old Testament focused both on God's provision for sin in the sacrificial system and also the celebration of God's covenant love and the deliverance of the chosen people from bondage. It is an engagement with God based on God's sovereign rule over our lives. There were both informal, ecstatic styles of worship (especially in the earlier period) and more formal, liturgical patterns. In both cases music was widely utilised (and possibly borrowed from pagan sources) and was believed to have real spiritual power when used in connection with the words of Scripture.

Some Questions

1. What are some examples of both "ecstatic" and "formal" worship styles in the church today? Which approach is typical of your own local church and in what way? Are there perhaps elements of both?

2. Though we no longer have animal sacrifices in our worship, what are some of the ways that atonement for sin is still a theological focus in our worship? We no longer bring the offering of a calf or of grain or oil. What sacrifice do we now bring?

3. Do you think it is proper to borrow secular music styles for use in worship? What is gained from this? Are there any dangers involved in this approach?

4. In what way might the Old Testament concept of "intimacy with God" differ from our own understanding of that expression?

5. How does the Exodus from Egypt have a parallel with elements of our own worship services?

6. How does the role of today's pastor or priest in leading worship differ from and at the same time have some continuity with the priests of the Old Testament?

Further Reading

Dyrness, William. *Themes in Old Testament Theology*. Downers Grove: Illinois / Exeter: Paternoster, 1997, especially the chapter on worship, pp. 143-59.

Hustad, Donald P. *Jubilate II: Church Music in Worship and Renewal*. Carol Stream: Hope Publishing, 1993.

Peterson, David. *Engaging with God: A Biblical Theology of Worship*. IVP Academic, 2002.

Saliers, Don E. *Music and Theology*. Nashville: Abingdon, 2007.

Waltke, Bruce W. and James M. Houston. *The Psalms as Christian Worship: An Historical Commentary*. Grand Rapids: Eerdmans, 2010.

CHAPTER THREE

Worship in the New Testament

A Note of Fulfilment

In the New Testament, worship is the celebration of the new world that God has brought into being through the birth, life, death, resurrection, and ascension of Jesus Christ. There is a note of fulfilment in all of this. The old *cultus* is done away with and a new and living way has opened up before humanity. Some have seen this as implying the doing away with any idea of holy people, places or things. Now all of creation is, at least potentially, made holy through the offering up of the body of Jesus Christ once, for all.[1] Others have argued that the holiness of Christian "things" far from being something abolished by the Incarnation of Christ are the means of God's connecting with the world.[2]

> God's holiness as it is known in Jesus Christ is not purity and arrogant distance but unity with all the needy world. The Christian faith trusts that the very signs at the heart of the assembly, the signs of word and meal and bath as these have been transformed in Christ, are gifts of God which communicate that holiness as an alternative vision of the world.[3]

In either case, it remains that the new world inaugurated in the coming of Christ is announced in the church's proclamation – in all that Christians do and say as they gather for worship. In the Old Testament the presence of God was something that would fall upon the people under certain prescribed conditions. When everything was done properly in the tabernacle and temple worship, the glory of God might descend like a cloud upon the congregation. However a New Testament model of worship is different because the assumption is that God is already present as we gather. In fact the Greek word translated "church" is *ekklesia* - "the called out ones." We have only assembled because God has called us and drawn us together. We have no need to "call down" the presence of God but rather to recognise and announce it.

Of course this does not rule out the place of "invocation." To call upon God to act in the present is certainly appropriate. The action of God in the present

1   David Peterson, *Engaging with God: A Biblical Theology of Worship* (Leicester: Apollos, 1992).
2   See Gordon Lathrop's trilogy *Holy Things: A Liturgical Theology* (Minneapolis: Augsburg Fortress, 1998); *Holy People: A Liturgical Ecclesiology* (Minneapolis: Augsburg Fortress, 1999); *Holy Ground: A Liturgical Cosmology* (Minneapolis: Augsburg Fortress, 2009).
3   Gordon W. Lathrop, *Holy Things*, cited by Byron D. Stuhlman, *Christian Century* 28 July, 1999.

emerges, however, out of his saving work in Jesus Christ and is not something generated by ourselves. There are well meaning Christians who strive to find some key to experiencing "anointed" worship or the "shekinah glory" or some other ecstatic experience in worship and attempt to bring it about, often through worship "techniques" or even crowd manipulation. But what would be the point of seeking such an experience when we have Jesus himself in our midst? The New Testament teaches us that in him we see "the glory as of a father's only son, full of grace and truth." (John 1:14) Many believers have been taught to anticipate a certain kind of peak experience in worship, have perhaps been trying to obtain it and may be quite put off by my suggestion that such a search is futile and ill advised. I have known people who have driven themselves to depression and worse by worrying themselves about finding a certain spiritual ecstasy in their worship. They become critical of their pastors, their worship leaders, and even of themselves looking for someone to blame for why their experience of worship is not as "anointed" as it should be. There is something very liberating about finding in the New Testament a note of *fulfilment*. Everything that can be done to bring us to God has already been done for us by Jesus. It is certainly appropriate to call down the glory of God or evoke God's presence through our praises, our music, our songs and our ritual acts, but such actions do not manipulate an unwilling God. God is already present before we gather. What we do in our liturgy is recognise (not bring about) that Presence, and announce and celebrate what God has done through the finished work of Jesus Christ.

The Theology of Sunday

There is a deep theology behind the very day on which we meet. Some may think it is merely a tradition that we meet on Sunday, the first day of the week. Others are under the misapprehension that Sunday worship has something to do with the Emperor Constantine introducing pagan ideas to the fourth century church that presaged a falling away from an earlier purity. In fact the church since the earliest times has very deliberately met on the first day of the week to commemorate the resurrection of Christ from the dead and the choice of the day is deeply grounded in New Testament concepts. In the "theology of Sunday" we learn to mark time according to God's redemptive actions.[4] There is in fact a kind of Trinitarian shape to the theology of Sunday, for creation began on the first day of the week, Christ was raised from the dead on the first day of the week, and the Spirit was given at Pentecost on the first day of the week. Christians have sometimes kept Sunday as a kind of "Christian Sabbath" as if it were a day of rest along the lines of the Jewish

---

4   Adrian Nocent OSB, *The Liturgical Year: Sundays in Ordinary Time* (Collegeville, MN: Order of St. Bendict, 1977), 9-19.

Sabbath. However, where the Sabbath commemorates God's rest from creation and his covenant with Israel, the Christian "Lord's Day" celebrates not rest but new creation. Some of the early Christian writers spoke of Sunday as the "eighth day" because it brought into being a whole new deal for humanity and indeed for the entire universe. Christ conquered sin, hell, and death on the first day of the week ushering in a new age – the Gospel age. Though there are many important feasts in the Church's worship, such as Christmas, Easter, and Pentecost, Sunday takes precedence over them all, for all other celebrations derive from the Sunday celebration which commemorates the central event on the Christian calendar. Every Sunday is a mini-Easter. Better still, every Easter is a big Sunday.

New Testament Vocabulary of Worship

There are a number of Greek New Testament words that are translated "worship" or that are related to the idea of worship. We can learn much about worship by examining them in their context.

> *Proskeunein* - "to fall down before, to prostrate, like a dog licks the hand of its master." In Matthew 4:10 and Luke 4:8 Jesus makes it clear that this is to be offered to God alone. In Hebrews 1:6 we are told that "when [God] brings the firstborn [Christ] into the world, he says, 'Let all God's angels worship him.'" This worship is described also in Revelation 4:10 where "the twenty-four elders fall before the one who is seated on the throne, and worship the one who lives forever and ever." John 4:21-24 tells us that this worship is to be offered "in spirit and truth."

> *Sebomai* – "to revere, to adore." In Matthew 15:9 the Pharisees were rebuked by Jesus for offering worship in vain. According to Acts 18:13, Paul was accused by some Jewish leaders at Corinth of persuading the people "to worship God in ways that are contrary to the law."

> *Latruein* – "to minister, to serve." Worship involves the consecration of the whole person, as is clear in Paul's exhortation to the Romans to present their bodies as "a living sacrifice, holy and acceptable to God" an offering described as their "spiritual worship."(Romans 12:1) In Philippians 3:3 believers are urged to "worship" or "serve" the Lord "by [or "in"] the Spirit."

A Brief Corinthian Case Study

A study of just one passage of scripture (1 Corinthians chs 11-14) provides us with some important New Testament principles of worship. Worship is not only directed upward toward God but also outward toward others, in that it must "edify" (build up) the congregation. Gifts are to be tested by this criterion and regulated accordingly (1 Cor. 14:26). Worship is not a chaotic mess of spontaneous expressions but must be formed and ordered in keeping with the character of God, who is not the "author of confusion but of peace" (1 Cor. 14:33 KJV). Appropriate attire for worship is based on a principle of culturally determined decorum (11:2-16). In the New Testament period this meant head coverings for women, though this rule cannot be made to apply in all contexts, where differing culturally-determined standards of modesty prevail. Behaviour at the Lord's Supper is to be based on the principle of orderly and reverent recognition of Christ's presence in the body and on regard for the needs of others (11:17-34). Spiritual gifts, while beneficial, are worthless if not accompanied by love (ch. 13). Worship must be intelligible if it is to build community and so the gift of languages must always be accompanied by interpretation (14:27 ff).

Music in the New Testament

There are no musical instruments mentioned in connection with Christian worship in the New Testament (this doesn't mean that none were used; only that we have no reference to such use). However, the New Testament is full of singing. The Gospel story opens with the song of angels – "Glory to God in the highest heaven, and on earth peace among those whom he favours!"(Luke 2:14) Christians have much to sing about and the joy of salvation has always found expression in music and song.

The Great Canticles

The chief source of New Testament and early church music was the Psalms. Certain New Testament texts, known as "canticles" were also adopted early and used in the liturgy. The majority of New Testament scholars believe that these passages pre-existed as sung hymns in Christian congregations before they found their way into the Scriptures. Their names are drawn from the first words of their Latin versions.

1. The *Magnificat* (Mary's Song) – Luke 1:46-55, "My soul magnifies the Lord..."
2. The *Benedictus* (Zechariah's Song) – Luke 1:68-79, "Blessed be the Lord God of Israel..."
3. The *Gloria in Excelsis* (the Angels' Song) – Luke 2:14, "Glory to God in the highest heaven..."
4. The *Nunc Dimittis* (Simeon's Song) – Luke 2:29, "Master you are dismissing your servant in peace…"

"Psalms, Hymns, and Spiritual Songs"

The expression "psalms, hymns, and spiritual songs" occurs twice in the Pauline literature (Col. 3:16; Eph. 5:19). "Psalms" is clearly a reference to the Jewish Psalter. "Hymns" were probably new songs that expressed the Christology of the early church. Fragments of early Christian hymns in the New Testament may include 1 Timothy 3:16; 2 Timothy 2:11-13; Ephesians 5:14; and Philippians 2:6-11. "Spiritual songs" may have been spontaneous songs as an extension of the "alleluia" at the end of a chant, or something more like the singing in a charismatic service today, though whether it is a reference to "singing in tongues" is uncertain. Augustine of Hippo, in the fifth century, spoke about the practice of what he called "jubilation." It sounds a little like the "tongues speaking" heard in charismatic worship today, though it may well be something else. "It is a certain sound of joy without words…it is the expression of a mind poured forth in joy…A person rejoicing in…certain words which cannot be…understood, bursts forth into sounds of exultation without words so that it seems he, filled with excessive joy cannot express in words the subject of that joy."[5]

Instrumental Music in the New Testament

As noted earlier, the New Testament is unfortunately silent about the use of musical instruments in worship, though it is hard to believe that when Psalms were sung in Gentile congregations no one ever brought along any instruments for accompaniment. We know that instrumental music was phased out of Jewish synagogue worship during the Second Temple period, because of its association with both pagan worship and the worship of heretical Jewish sects. By the time of Christ, only stringed instruments were used in Temple worship. After the destruction of the Second Temple in 70 CE, all instrumental music in the synagogues ceased. Though throughout history some churches have banned the use of instrumental music in worship, it is important to remember that there is neither prescription *nor* prohibition of their use in the New Testament.

The Function of Music in the New Testament.

James 5:15 urges singing as an expression of joy. Paul expresses a concern, in 1 Cor. 14:15, that singing be both spiritual and intellectual. Songs are a teaching device according to Col. 3:16 (though altered punctuation might change the meaning of this verse). Hebrews 13:15 urges "through [Jesus]… let us continually offer a sacrifice of praise to God, that is, the fruit of the lips that confess his name." Praise songs certainly enable this activity. Eph 5:19b

---

5   Augustine, "Expositions on the Book of Psalms," *Nicene and Post-Nicene Fathers* Series 1 (Peabody, MA: Hendrickson, 1995) 8: 488.

and Col. 3:16b remind us that making melody to the Lord is an expression of the heart.

An Application to Our Worship Today

Does singing still have a place in the church? Most Christians would feel that a service of worship would be incomplete if it did not include singing. Yet some, including some in the "emerging church" movement, have questioned the usefulness or appropriateness of singing in a world in which fewer people seem to attend church and are less familiar with community singing or with the church's musical tradition. Two ideas often expressed are 1) that congregational singing is a cultural construct and thus not a biblically mandated aspect of worship, and 2) that public singing is not a part of contemporary culture. The conclusion drawn from these premises is that we should consider minimising the amount of congregational singing in our services, since the average person would find such activity either meaningless or uncomfortable.

In answer to the first point, there are a number of biblical references that do indeed seem to mandate congregational singing. The Psalms are full of exhortations for the people of God to sing. These take the form, in the most part, of commands. In fact, the Book of Psalms was the songbook of ancient Israel; it is a liturgical document – a songbook. Of what use is a songbook if it is not intended to be a book from which people sing? The command of the author of the letter to the Colossians that they should "with gratitude in your hearts sing psalms, hymns, and spiritual songs, to God" (Col. 3:16) is repeated in almost identical words to the Ephesian church, only there the congregational nature of the singing is made more evident as the exhortations includes the instruction to sing such songs "among yourselves" (Eph. 5:19). Clearly this is congregational singing. As noted above, most New Testament scholars are in agreement that certain passages in the New Testament are in fact fragments of early hymns, providing a fascinating insight into the liturgy of the earliest Christians. These passages include the so-called "kenosis" passage of Philippians 2:1-10, and the great creedal songs of 1 Timothy 2:5, 1 Timothy 3:16, and 2 Timothy 2:11-13. It is for this reason that most modern translations set these kinds of passages off in "poetic" indentation – to make their literary type clear. One of the earliest secular witnesses to what Christians did when they came together says that Christians gathered early on the morning of the first day of the week, "to sing songs to Christ as to a god."[6] The vast majority of congregations have continued this practice down to the present time. Joseph Gelineau has argued that singing takes an

---

6   Pliny, "Epistle X (ad Trajan)," xcvi, cited in Henry Bettensen, *Documents of the Christian Church* (London: Oxford University Press, 1959), 4-5.

undifferentiated crowd and turns it into an ordered Christian congregation. We ought not to reduce singing to a kind of churchy karaoke![7]

Nothing could be more destructive to the nature of true worship than the proposal given by some that churches should dispense with congregational singing and instead sing *to* the congregation, allowing the individual in the congregation to sing along only if they want to – more like in a rock concert performance. The problem here is that this strikes at the principle that worship is to be the *work of the people*. It is to be *participatory* if it is to achieve its desired end of glorifying God and building up the body of Christ.[8] Two historical examples of a "spectator" approach to worship come to mind at this point. One is the Medieval Mass during which the priest performed a rite before the congregation, while the people sat as mute spectators. Another is drawn from nineteenth century Protestantism, especially in America, where paid choirs were often hired to sing to the congregation as they sat down and passively listened. One of the great aspects of worship renewal in more contemporary times, among both Protestants and Catholics, has been the insistence on a *participatory* form of worship in which, not just the clergy, or other "professionals", but all the people of God have their role to play. There will always be those who can't sing or won't sing in our worship services. We need not interfere with these people or make them feel badly. Just because they feel that they "can't sing" (and most people who *feel* that way actually don't sing too badly) doesn't mean that they do not participate in and enjoy congregational singing at some level.

Now to the second assertion – that group singing is foreign to contemporary culture. I am convinced that this is not in fact the case, but for argument's sake let's assume it is. One might well ask, "So what?" So are activities such as praying, reading the Bible, taking bread and wine in remembrance of Christ's death and immersing people in water in the Name of the Triune God. Does that mean we should quit doing such things? These are at least as "alien," and some are more so, to the average person, than group singing. We do "the average person" (whatever that means in a world as culturally diverse as ours) a great disservice when we assume that he or she knows nothing about religious activity or what is likely to happen in a church service. They may not understand the precise meaning of the acts they observe in a typical church on a Sunday morning (nor would many Christians for that matter),

---

7   I am grateful to Robert Gribben for this insight. See Jones, Wainwright, Yarnold and Bradshaw, eds. *The Study of the Liturgy* (London: SPCK,), 493ff.

8   The participatory nature of worship has been identified by Stephen Burns as a key theme of worship for the Uniting Church in Australia. Stephen Burns, *Pilgrim People: An Introduction to Worship in the Uniting Church* (Adelaide: MediaCom, 2012), 19-20.

but they are not stupid. I would say that, at least in my own Australian context, the "average person" who is not a Christian would enter a worship service knowing that there would be some things they would not understand, and some religious behaviours with which they were not going to be as familiar as a regular worshipper. They would *expect* this and probably bring with them a natural curiosity, and may even find the "strangeness" appealing and worth investigating. If a visitor receives a loving welcome from a community of transformed individuals expressing the love of Christ, the "style" of worship will not be a problem to them. If they do not receive such a welcome, then no amount of "seeker sensitivity" is going to make them feel at ease.

One is sometimes given the impression that all cultures are to be respected except the church's own culture. Is the church to be a culture-free zone? Clearly not. There are aspects of church culture, such as prayer, hymn singing and sacramental practice, which are completely foreign to some secularised people who have not grown up with any Christian influence. Yet these same people have often received this church culture as a gift, passed on by others who loved it and saw its abiding value. I am grateful to God that these were not dispensed with by those who nurtured me into the faith from a non-church background. Might it be that aspects of our own church culture that are truly beneficial might be being sacrificed in the name of being "contemporary," to the loss of future generations? Nor is it the case that group singing is always culturally foreign. Carols by Candlelight is one grass roots movement among ordinary Australians that seems to show no sign of abating in popularity. Plenty of group singing goes on in pubs, around the piano of many a living room, and around many a campfire in the bush on camping trips. Hymns, music, and song are vital aspects of our tradition and a priceless heritage given to us to share with the rest of the church and with the whole world. Newer songs must by all means be welcomed but these should supplement and add to the existing musical treasures of the church, not replace them.

Summary

The New Testament strikes a note of fulfilment which is reflected in the Church's worship. God in Christ has reconciled sinners and ushered in a new creation. The Church comes together to worship because it is called out to do so by God. It gathers around the Risen Christ, graced by the Spirit. The use of Sunday as the day of worship is not just a tradition but has behind it a deep theo-logic, for it was on this day that God raised Jesus from the dead and ushered in a new deal for humanity. Christian worship first glorifies God but it also edifies believers, and the use of spiritual gifts in the context of worship must always be for the good of the whole community. Worship involves drawing near to God, reverencing God and serving God. While there is no reference in the New Testament to the use of musical instruments in worship, singing is encouraged as a means of expressing joy and professing belief.

Some Questions

1. Why is it important to give the New Testament priority over the Old Testament in planning our worship services? What are some of the things that can happen when this is not the case?

2. We often call our time of gathering for worship a "service." Is there any New Testament foundation for doing this?

3. What do you think of the claim that congregational singing should be eliminated from our worship services?

4. How are musical instruments used in worship in your own congregation?

5. Worship is certainly a spiritual activity, but this doesn't mean that it is not also something physical and embodied. How is worship "embodied" in your congregation?

6. How do the things we do in worship function as "signs" of the reign of God and of the story of salvation?

For Further Reading:

Johansson, Calvin M. *Discipling Music Ministry: Twenty-First Century Directions*. Peabody: Hendrickson, 1992.

Gordon Lathrop, *Holy Things: A Liturgical* Theology. Minneapolis: Augsburg Fortress, 1998.

___. *Holy People: A Liturgical Ecclesiology*. Minneapolis: Augsburg Fortress, 1999.

___. *Holy Ground: A Liturgical Cosmology*. Minneapolis: Augsburg Fortress, 2009.

Martin, Ralph P. *Worship in the Early Church*. Grand Rapids: Eerdmans, 1964.

Peterson, David. *Engaging with God: A Biblical Theology of Worship*. Leicester: Apollos, 1992.

Wren, Brian. *Praying Twice: The Music and Words of Congregational Song*. Louisville: Westminster / John Knox Press, 2000.

Chapter Four

Worship in the Early Church: From Synagogue to Ecclesia

The First and Second Centuries

We noted in the last chapter that the early church borrowed the pattern of synagogue worship, with its simple service of prayer, praise, and scriptural reading and commentary, and then added its distinctively Christian content.[1] Christians were the *ecclesia* (the Greek word which we translate as "church") - the "called out ones"- who had responded to God's electing grace and were gathered together to celebrate the salvation that was theirs in Christ. The Roman governor, Pliny, in writing to the emperor Trajan around 112 AD, to seek advice on how he should treat those who had been arrested on the charge of being Christian, gave a brief description of the way Christians worshipped at that time. It is an important pagan reference to early Christian worship.

> They declared that the sum of their guilt or error had amounted only to this, that on an appointed day they had been accustomed to meet before daybreak, and to recite a hymn antiphonally to Christ, as to a god, and to bind themselves by an oath, not for the commission of any crime but to abstain from theft, robbery, adultery and breach of faith, and not to deny a deposit when it was claimed. After the conclusion of this ceremony it was their custom to depart and meet again to take food; but it was ordinary and harmless food, and they had ceased this practice after my edict in which, in accordance with your orders, I had forbidden secret societies. I thought it the more necessary, therefore, to find out what truth there was in this by applying torture to two maidservants, who were called deaconesses. But I found nothing but a depraved and arrogant superstition, and I therefore postponed my examination and had recourse to you for consultation.[2]

As noted in chapter 3, since New Testament times Christians have worshipped on the first day of the week, Sunday, which they refer to as "the Lord's Day." This was the day upon which Christ had been raised from the dead, so each

---

1   The typology I have used for dividing time periods in this and the following chapters ("From Synagogue to Ecclessia, from Ecclesia to Temple, from Temple to Auditorium, from Auditorium to Tent") is taken from memory from a lecture given by Robert Webber at Asbury Theological Seminary in 1997 or 1998 and may be slightly inaccurate. "From Tent to Kaleidoscope" is my own addition.

2   Pliny, "Epistle X (ad Trajan)," xcvi, cited in Henry Bettensen, *Documents of the Christian Church* (London: Oxford University Press, 1959), 4-5.

Sunday was of special significance. In the first century church there were actually two Lord's Day meetings. Since the earliest followers of Jesus were Jews, they continued for a time to worship on the Sabbath (Saturday) and then to gather again on the first day of the week (Sunday) to celebrate the resurrection. The morning service (pre-dawn or at dawn) was made up of a simple synagogue-like service of scripture reading, exhortation by the leading presbyter (elder), prayers and singing. Then a second service was held, in the evening, the *agape* (love feast), which was a Eucharistic service, with Holy Communion as its central focus. By the second century the "love feast" had been dropped, and the Eucharist had been brought into the morning service. Justin Martyr (c. 100-165) in his *First Apology* gives a fascinating description of the worship of this period. The fact that Christians met in secret gave rise to much suspicion. What was a "love feast"? Was it some kind of sexual orgy? What does it mean when Christians say that they eat the flesh and drink the blood of their founder? Are they cannibals? Christians kept quiet for the most part, but Justin was the first to come right out into the open with the pagans and describe exactly what it was that Christians did behind closed doors. He describes baptism and how the newly baptized are brought to their first communion. Bread, and wine mixed with water are brought to the presbyter, who offers thanks for them to the Trinity. After this prayer, the congregation responds with "Amen." The deacons then distribute the bread and wine to those assembled, and also to those who are absent.

> This food we call Eucharist, of which no one is allowed to partake except one who believes that the things we teach are true, and has received the washing for forgiveness of sins and for rebirth, and who lives as Christ handed down to us. For we do not receive these things as common bread or common drink; but as Jesus Christ our Savior being incarnate by God's word took flesh and blood for our salvation, so also we have been taught that the food consecrated by the word of prayer which comes from him, from which our flesh and blood are nourished by transformation, is the flesh and blood of that Incarnate Jesus.[3]

Justin then speaks of the Gospels as the "memoirs" of the Apostles and recounts Jesus' words of institution, given in the Last Supper as recounted

---

3 'The First Apology of Justin Martyr,' translated by Edward R. Hardy in *Early Christian Fathers* (Philadelphia: Westminster, 1953). 276-88, cited in Hugh T. Kerr, *Readings in Christian Thought* (Nashville: Abingdon Press, 1990), 22-24. Though this may sound in some respects like the much later Catholic doctrine of "transubstantiation" it is important not to confuse the two. Justin is using the analogical language typical of his day, and we should not read later debates on the Lord's Supper, for example those between Protestants and Catholics in the sixteenth century, back into this earlier period.

by Paul in 1 Corinthians 11:23-25 ("This is my body…this is my blood…Do this in remembrance of me"). After these services, the Christians are said to "constantly remind each other of these things." Justin also gives instructions concerning the offering. "Those who prosper, and who so wish, contribute, each one as much as he chooses to. What is collected is deposited with the president, and he takes care of orphans and widows, and those who are in want on account of sickness or any other cause…"[4]

One is struck in this description by the great similarity between the early church's worship practices and those that have continued until today.

- They met on the first day of the week. Contrary to the claims of some Adventist groups that the early Christians did not meet on Sunday until Constantine decreed Sunday a day of worship in the fourth century, Justin makes it clear in this early second century source, that Sunday, not the Jewish Saturday Sabbath, was the Christian day of worship. "We all hold this common gathering on Sunday," he writes, "since it is the first day, on which God transforming darkness and matter made the universe, and Jesus Christ rose from the dead on the same day. For they crucified him on the day before Saturday, and on the day after Saturday, he appeared to his apostles and disciples and taught them these things which I have passed on to you for your consideration."[5]
- The Gospels are read, and/or the Old Testament, by a "reader."
- The presbyter [elder or pastor] then gives a sermon, "a discourse urging the imitation of these noble things."
- Prayers are offered from a standing position, the stance of the resurrection.[6]
- The Lord's Supper is celebrated.
- A free will offering is taken, and proportional giving [from "those who prosper"] is accepted, and distributed to those in need.

All of the above actions remain the practice of most churches to this day.

We now consider one final ancient source on the worship of the early church. *The Didache* ["Teaching"] is an anonymous source not discovered until 1873 but believed by most scholars either to be the oldest surviving piece of Christian literature outside of the New Testament, or at very least to date as

---

4   'The First Apology of Justin Martyr,' in Kerr, 23-24.

5   *The First Apology of Justin Martyr*, Kerr, 24.

6   This is still the practice in Orthodox churches today and in Evangelical Protestant churches in parts of the world where Orthodoxy has been historically widespread, indicating a continuation of the practice from earliest times.

early as the mid-second century.[7] It discusses baptismal practices, insisting that baptism should be "in the Name of the Father, and of the Son, and of the Holy Spirit." Baptism should be by immersion in running water, if possible, otherwise by immersion in ordinary (standing) water. If immersion is not possible, sprinkling water on the head three times in the Triune Name is acceptable. Fasting should precede baptism.[8] The praying of the Lord's Prayer three times a day is urged upon believers. A sample of a Eucharistic prayer is given, and the insistence that only the baptized should partake. This is a formal, written, prayer, but it is also interesting to note that "prophets should be free to give thanks as they please." This indicates that there was a place both for formal liturgical prayers, and for spontaneous extemporary prayers. These were not considered, as they sometimes are today, to be mutually exclusive forms of prayer.

Regulations for the use of the spiritual gifts of travelling missionaries or evangelists are then given, designed to weed out impostors and charlatans. "If any charismatist [prophet], speaking in a trance, says 'Give me money (or anything else)', do not listen to him. On the other hand, if he bids you give it to someone else who is in need, nobody should criticize him."[9] One wonders how some of today's televangelists would get on if this rule continued to be in force.

Tithing is urged as the method of giving, and the day of worship is said to be "the Lord's Day" and to include the celebration of the Eucharist, preceded by confession of sins and reconciliation between offended parties. "Overseers" [bishops] and "assistants" [deacons] are to be chosen from among the congregation, on the basis of character qualities, and are to be held in high regard. Finally, "In your prayers, your almsgiving, and everything you do, be guided by what you read in the Gospel of our Lord."[10]

The Third and Fourth Centuries

The earliest liturgical writings speak of "presbyters" and "deacons" and their roles in worship. By the third century, we see the development of the Episcopal system of a "three-fold order" of bishops, priests, and deacons. The presbyters

---

7   "The Didache," translated by Maxwell Staniforth, in *Early Christian Writings: The Apostolic Fathers* (Harmondsworth: Penguin, 1981), 225-37. For a more recent translation see Aaron Milevic, *The Didache: Text, Translation, Analysis and Commentary* (Collegeville: MN: Michael Glazier, 2004). See also William Varner, *The Way of the Didache: The First Christian Handbook* (Lanham, MD: University Press of America, 2007).

8   "The Didache," *Early Christian Writings: The Apostolic Fathers*, 230-31.

9   "The Didache," *Early Christian Writings: The Apostolic Fathers*, 233. The word "charismatist" is the translator's choice and a rather clumsy one. The Greek could be translated simply as "prophet."

10   "The Didache," *Early Christian Writings: The Apostolic Fathers*, 234-5.

began to be seen less as teachers and preachers, and more as stewards of the "mysteries" [sacraments] of God. Baptism was usually performed at Easter, after a lengthy period of preparation, including fasting. Those preparing for baptism were called "catechumens" and were increasingly separated from the baptised worshippers, congregating in a separate section of the church and being dismissed before the Communion service.

Early Christians in Rome sometimes met in underground burial chambers (catacombs), where they also interred their dead. These were made up of miles of passages, twenty to fifty feet below ground. After Constantine's Edict of Milan in 313, guaranteeing freedom of worship for Christians, worship became legal and congregations larger. Christians began to build their own places of worship based on the Roman basilica model. A basilica was an important civic gathering place, "a rectangular hall with a semi-circular niche or 'apse' opening off one of the shorter sides. Inside it was divided by two, and sometimes four, rows of columns into a wider central space and two or four parallel long narrow spaces…various forms of basilica were commonly built to accommodate crowds attending a law court, market or any kind of assembly."[11] Christians also used the *aula* a more humble 'meeting house', but it was the basilica which was their choice for the Sunday gathering.

It is true that the early Christians prior to this often met in homes, and the house church movement of today sees this as a worthy pattern to be followed. However, it should be noted that meeting in homes was a practical matter for the early Christians. Until they could be sure that they would not be subjected to further imperial persecution they needed to meet discreetly in private. Often the homes in which they met were the homes of wealthy members of the Christian community who had large enough rooms to accommodate crowds. Archaeological finds have uncovered evidence of the demolition of walls to create auditorium-like spaces within these homes. So the space within an early Christian "house church" functioned much more like that in a typical suburban church building today than to "house church" meetings marked by informality and a relaxed "homey" atmosphere. One major difference is that there were no pews. It is not known with certainty when pews were first introduced; it may have been as early as the thirteenth century. Not until the sixteenth century did they begin to dominate the worship space. Prior to this people stood throughout the entire liturgy and this is still the practice in most Orthodox churches today, though western influence has sometimes seen the use of pews creeping in.

---

11   Henry F. Sefton, "Building for Worship," in Tim Dowley, ed. *The History of Christianity: A Lion Handbook* (Oxford: Lion, 1990), 158-61.

The liturgy still included much extemporary prayer and exhortation by the local bishop, but worship patterns became increasingly more fixed. It is uncertain exactly when the "Words of Institution" at the Lord's Supper were introduced or understood as having divine authority attached to them.[12] They seem to have been understood in this sense first in the Eastern Church. Eventually they gained a more or less fixed shape, but with important regional variations.[13] The "Holy, Holy, Holy" of Isaiah 6 became widely incorporated into the Eucharist. Trinitarian doxologies began to appear at the end of prayers. Early creeds developed, arising out of the vows made at Baptism. The creed we now know as "The Apostles' Creed" originally began as a simple expression of praise and confession of the Lordship of Jesus Christ. By the second century, creeds were being used as a "symbol" or "rule of faith" for believers. Justin Martyr insisted on the candidate for baptism professing to believe and live by the truth. Irenaeus speaks of "the canon of truth which everyone received at his baptism." In both Hippolytus (early to mid-third century) and Tertullian we find descriptions of a three-fold dipping corresponding to a three-fold interrogation oriented around the three persons of the Trinity. The candidate replies *credo* ("I believe") after each question is put. In the fourth and fifth centuries this threefold interrogation began to be elaborated into a rudimentary creed.

Practices such as the burning of incense, the carrying of candles as a mark of honour, and the curtaining off of the altar, are thought by some to be pagan imports into the liturgy. However, it should also be noted that such practices are also found in the Old Testament, and that they may be viewed more positively as a successful enculturation of the Gospel. The Church Year became much more complex. Easter was extended into a weeklong festival (Holy Week), including Palm Sunday (commemorating Jesus' entry to Jerusalem on a donkey), Maundy Thursday (commemorating the Last Supper) and Good Friday (commemorating the death of Christ). Lent was established as a period of preparation for catechumens who were joined by others in the congregation in their journey toward baptism, which took place at Easter. It varied in length according to region and the preferences of the bishop but its final shape in the western tradition of forty days is drawn from the Bible. Today it is observed as a period (excluding Sundays) of fasting and self-denial in preparation for

---

12   The "words of institution" are the words of Christ spoken at the Last Supper as recorded in the Synoptic Gospels (Matthew 26:26-29; Mark 14:22-25; Luke 22:19-21); and Paul (I Corinthians 11:23-29). There are variations in the wording in the Gospels and the 'narrative' constructed from the passages for liturgical use is an attempted harmony.

13   For a collection of early Eucharistic prayers see Arthur Linton, *Twenty-Five Consecration Prayers with Notes and Introduction* (New York: SPCK, 1921).

Easter. Its origins in the catechumenate remind us that Lent is not entirely about penitence and self-renunciation but also about claiming and reclaiming our baptism.[14]

The celebration of Christmas Day was adopted around 350 CE, but was originally part of the much longer season of Epiphany. Christmas and Epiphany have a similar relationship as Lent and Easter.[15] Where the earliest liturgies were in Greek, by this period we read of Latin, Syriac, Coptic, and other language variants. Eventually Latin would replace Greek almost exclusively (at least in the West). Influential and powerful churches such as Rome did not make an attempt to enforce liturgical conformity, except in a few regions where administrative jurisdiction required it, leading to many regional differences and considerable diversity of practice.

Preaching was very popular in the fourth century, and some of the great preachers, such as John Chrysostom in the East and Ambrose in the West, would be cheered (and sometimes booed!) by their congregations. On one occasion, Chrysostom (whose name means "golden mouth") rebuked the congregation for applauding his performance as a preacher. He did it so eloquently that they responded by cheering him!

The fourth century was an age in which there was much controversy surrounding the nature of Jesus. An Alexandrian presbyter named Arius claimed that the Son of God was a created being and that there was a time when he did not exist. While the church had always believed that God was Father, Son, and Holy Spirit the "Arian" controversy led to the formal definition of the doctrine of the Trinity, and the insistence that Jesus was both fully human and fully divine. This whole controversy actually arose out of liturgical practice because the Arians were praying in ways that did not attribute full divinity to the Son, and they claimed that the Orthodox (those who opposed the Arians) did the same in their prayers. All of this contributed to the church's worship in a number of important ways.

The addition of the Nicene Creed to the Eucharist, whereas formerly its place had been more or less confined to the baptismal ritual was designed to ensure that the doctrine of Christ's full divinity was safeguarded. "As such the Nicene Creed became a mark of catholic and orthodox identity, but it was also deeply evangelical because it summarized the gospel story of Jesus."[16] The *Gloria Patri*

---

14   This insight comes courtesy of Professor Robert Gribben.

15   See "Year, Liturgical," in Paul Bradshaw, ed. *The New SCM Dictionary of Liturgy and Worship* (London: SCM Press, 2002).

16   Frank C. Senn, *Christian Liturgy: Catholic and Evangelical* (Minneapolis, MN: Fortress Press, 1997), 535.

["Glory be to the Father, and to the Son, and to the Holy Spirit…"] was revised so as to ensure a proper stress on the coequality of each Person of the Holy Trinity. There came a tendency to overstress the divine majesty of Christ, and his role as judge, at the expense of his humanity, and his role as redeemer, with a corresponding drop in the numbers attending the Eucharist, for fear of offending the Royal Host.

The festivals of Christmas and Epiphany became much more important because they stressed the Incarnation of Christ – the belief that in Jesus, God became human. Related to this was a much greater devotion to Mary in worship. She was referred to as *Theotokos* [the "God-Bearer"], and "the Mother of God." Protestants tend to think that the phrase "Mother of God" is saying something about Mary that shouldn't be said (as if the eternal God had been given birth to by another). But this actually misses the point of the early Christian use of this term where the stress was on the word "God." Mary was the mother of Jesus. Jesus was God incarnate, fully divine as well as fully human. Therefore, Mary was the mother of God. In the earlier period Mary was always associated with the doctrine of Christ, his divinity, and his Incarnation. Later, especially in Western Catholicism she began to take on special significance almost in her own right though the connection with the Incarnation was never lost. Eastern Orthodox icons of Mary always depict her with the Christ child, thereby preserving the strong link to the Incarnation.[17]

The Fifth and Sixth Centuries

These centuries see an increased distance between the Western Catholic and Eastern Orthodox wings of the Church. The East was generally more fixed in its liturgy, yet at the same time, allowed great regional diversity. No two Eucharistic services were identical, but there were certain more or less fixed elements. In both East and West, an increased number of festivals and saints days were added to the Church Calendar, so that it became very cluttered, challenging Sunday in importance. The spiritual efficacy of relics (the physical remains or supposed remains of apostles and saints) became increasingly more highly prized during this period and more and more fanciful legends of the miracles of the saints circulated. The division between clergy and laity was accentuated. The use of images and statues as aids to worship increased. Though the exact number of sacraments had not yet been formally defined, five in addition to Baptism and Eucharist began to emerge as having special significance– marriage, penance, ordination, confirmation, and extreme unction (anointing with oil, usually

---

17   See more detailed discussion of these features in Glen O'Brien, "The Effects of the Arian Controversy on the Liturgy of the Post-Nicene Church," *Aldersgate Papers* 3 (September 2002), 21-28.

in preparation for death). The Lord's Supper came increasingly to be viewed, almost exclusively, in terms of sacrifice, rather than as a memorial of Christ's sufferings, though both elements had been present from the earliest times. A strong connection between the power of the sacraments and the authority of priests emerged. If there was no priest there could be no Eucharist, and therefore no worship and no available grace. The veneration of Mary and of the saints meant that where prayers were once offered *through* them, now they began to be offered *to* them, such that they began to be seen as functioning as mediators between those in earth and those in heaven.

After most people had given up the Roman style of dress,[18] the priests continued to retain it, thus increasing the distance between clergy and laity. This should not be thought of as a medieval Catholic problem, however. When the Reformers later adopted the black academic preaching gown to stress their role as "doctors of sacred Scripture" they created just as effective a distance. Later the revivalists of the Great Awakenings set aside the black gown and adopted the "frock coat." The present use of the plain white linen alb in many churches may appear "priestly" to the untutored but is designed as a symbol not of ordination but of baptism and brings to mind the biblical image of white robed saints.[19]

Music in the Early Church

We noted earlier how the Younger Pliny of Bithynia wrote to the Emperor Trajan in 112 CE and described the coming together of Christians before daylight to sing hymns to Christ "as unto a god." So we know that the New Testament practice of sung music was continued in the worship of the early church. According to Osbeck, "The music of the earliest Christian churches was entirely vocal, with little regard for instruments of any kind. In fact, the early church fathers, such as Clement of Alexandria, Chrysostom, Ambrose, [and] Augustine, strongly denounced the use of instruments with sacred singing."[20] To this day there is no instrumental use in Orthodox churches. Clement of Alexandria in particular rejected any music associated with erotic dances. The melodies used should avoid certain intervals and be solemn and austere. All dancing was forbidden, and Chrysostom brought his considerable

---

18   Of course, until our own time, the poor wore only home-made garments, rags or hand-me-downs and had no formal dress to indicate their status.

19   It is the stole (the long scarf that hangs over the neck and down the front of the alb) which serves the function of indicating the role of the presbyter. For a helpful discussion of the history of and rationale for liturgical vestments see Robert Gribben, "Liturgical Dress in the Uniting Church." http://assembly.uca.org.au/worship/resources/10-guidelines/28-liturgicaldress.html, accessed 9 May 2013.

20   Osbeck, *Ministry of Music*, 20.

preaching ability to bear in opposing it. One exception to this is in the Ethiopian Orthodox Church which claims continuity with the ancient Jewish Temple worship in its stately dances performed in liturgical dress accompanied by drums, the voices of the choir and the hand-held percussive *sistrum*.

Synagogue chants and antiphonal (responsive) chants were adopted early. Ambrose, the fourth century Bishop of Milan did much to encourage congregational singing and is associated with "Ambrosian Chant" which was a forerunner to the better known "Gregorian Chant." He was concerned especially with combating Arianism through protest hymns. Some did oppose music all together, but for the most part it was encouraged. Augustine remembered how moving he found the Psalm chants in use in Milan, but was concerned that he might be guilty of the grave fault of finding the music more important to him than the words.

Following are some examples of early Christian hymns, which give us some idea of their lyrical content. Sadly their musical style is much more difficult to ascertain.

An Early Christian Antiphonal Chant

Christ is risen: the world below is in ruins.
Christ is risen: the spirits of evil are fallen.
Christ is risen: the angels of God are rejoicing.
Christ is risen: the tombs are void of their dead.
Christ indeed has arisen from the dead,
the first of the sleepers.
Glory and power are his forever.
Amen.[21]

An Early Christian Hymn

May none of God's wonderful works keep silence, night and morning.
Bright stars, high mountains, the depths of the seas, sources of rushing rivers:
May all these break into song as we sing to Father, Son, and Holy Spirit.
May all the angels in the heavens reply: Amen! Amen! Amen!
Power, praise, honour, eternal glory to God, the only giver of grace.
Amen! Amen! Amen!

---

21   This and the following samples of early Christian hymns are drawn from *Christian History Magazine* Issue 37, "Worship in the Early Church" edition, 1993.

"Shepherd of Tender Youth" - An Alexandrian Hymn (c. 190 AD)

Bridle-bit of untamed colts,
Wing of birds that do not go astray,
Sure Tiller of ships,
Shepherd of the King's lambs!
Gather your children who live in simplicity.
Let them sing in holiness.
Let them celebrate with sincerity,
With a mouth that knows no evil,
The Christ who guides his children!
O King of the saints,
O sovereign Word of the Most High Father,
Prince of wisdom,
Support of toiling men,
Eternal joy of the human family,
O Jesus, Saviour

Summary

Though many people today tell us that "we need to get back to worshipping the way the early church did" one is struck by reading accounts of worship in the first few centuries with how very similar it all seems to what still takes place in the typical church in today's world. There is prayer, singing, the reading and teaching of scripture, the Lord's Supper, an offering, and words of blessing to conclude, the whole service being overseen by an "up-front" leader. The degree of continuity found in these elements across time is quite striking. This not to say that there was no change at all. Worship became much more formal over time, the earlier simple worship of the synagogue format being replaced by an atmosphere more like the ancient temple worship or the pageantry of the Roman imperial court. There was a shift "from synagogue to ecclesia" and, as we shall see, from "ecclesia to temple."

Some Questions

1. Imagine a non-churched person has asked you, "Why do Christians worship on Sunday and not on some other day?" How might you answer them?

2. Does it surprise you that the basic pattern of worship doesn't seem to have changed much over two thousand years? Do you see this as a good thing? Why or why not?

3. What value is there in the use of theological affirmations, such as the Apostles' and Nicene Creeds, in worship?

4. The pattern of the early church's worship was clearly two-fold – the Service of the Word (preaching and teaching) was followed by the Service of the Table (Holy Communion). Why do you think this is not always the case today? What has contributed to the separation of these two things?

5. People are sometimes baptised today outside of the regular worship service, either in a private service for family and friends (in the case of some infant baptisms) or at a camp or some outdoor location.[22] Are there any reasons that might be given against this practice?

For Further Reading

Bradshaw, Paul. *The Search for the Origins of Christian Worship: Sources and Methods for the Study of Early Liturgy*. London: SPCK, 2002.

Chadwick, Henry. *The Early Church* (Harmondsworth: Penguin, 1993), ch. 18, "Worship and Art," 258-84.

Christian History Magazine Issue 37, "Worship in the Early Church," 1993.

Hurtado, Larry W. *At the Origins of Christian Worship: The Context and Character of Earliest Christian Devotion*. Grand Rapids: Eerdmans. 1999.

Johnson, Lawrence J. *Worship in the Early Church: An Anthology of Historical Sources*. 4 volumes. Collegeville, MN: Liturgical Press, 2010.

O'Brien, Glen "The Effects of the Arian Controversy on the Liturgy of the Post-Nicene Church," *Aldersgate Papers* 3 (September 2002), 21-28.

Wainwright, Geoffrey and Karen B. Westerfield-Tucker, eds. *The Oxford History of Christian Worship*. New York: Oxford University Press, 2005.

---

22   Though it sometimes still occurs, the practice of private baptisms is virtually ruled out in the Uniting Church. The best instructed Roman Catholic, Anglican and Lutheran clergy ensure that baptisms always take place in the context of the Sunday liturgy.

CHAPTER FIVE

Worship in the Middle Ages: From Ecclesia to Temple

The term 'Middle Ages' was first coined about 1669 by Christopher Keller (1638-1707) who thought of three divisions in the history of the West. According to his scheme ancient history (the classical world of Greece and Rome so greatly admired by Renaissance men like Keller) ended in 325. Modern history began in 1453 when the fall of Constantinople brought a flood of Greek scholars and manuscripts to the West, initiating the Renaissance period. The years in between he called the "Middle" ages, because they appeared to him to be sterile through the absence of classical learning. Since then some scholars have designated the earlier half (c.500-1000) as the 'Dark Ages.' Older thinkers have thought of this period as a dark night between the light of classical Greece and the rise of renaissance humanism. More recent thought however has uncovered a rich though gradual development in culture and learning throughout the whole of the medieval period, and particularly the second half.

> The history of the Western church in the Middle Ages is the history of the most elaborate and thoroughly integrated system of religious thought and practice the world has ever known...The identification of the church with the whole of organised society is the fundamental feature which distinguishes the Middle Ages from earlier and later periods of history.[1]

The medieval period tends to be viewed according to two extremes. Either it is a great golden age when the Church was at the peak of its glory, strength and majesty, or it is a time of superstition, decline, false doctrine and idolatry. Neither view is accurate, for like any period it had high and low moments. The Yale historian George Parker Fisher described the social cohesiveness of the medieval period. "Every thought on divine things, every aspiration, every fear, was bodied forth in symbols. Prayer and praise, religious ceremonies, sacred festivals and pageants, formed an atmosphere in which the entire community lived and breathed."[2]

Given that most Protestants tend to have a very negative view of the medieval period, often drawn from depictions given in popular culture, for the sake of balance I include here a very positive description provided by the nineteenth

---

1   R.W. Southern, *Western Society and the Church in the Middle Ages* (Harmondsworth: Penguin, 1970), 15-16.
2   George Park Fisher, *History of the Christian Church* (New York: Scribners, 1910), 229.

century Anglican priest, John Henry Newman, who famously converted to Roman Catholicism and became a Cardinal. Admittedly it is a rather idealised portrait (as can be Protestant portraits of the Reformation period), but one does sense the appeal of a "Christian Europe" such as is described here.

> The fair form of Christianity rose up and grew and expanded like a beautiful pageant, from north to south; it was majestic, it was solemn, it was bright, it was beautiful and pleasant, it was soothing to the griefs, it was indulgent to the hopes of man; it was at once a teaching and a worship; it had a dogma, a mystery, a ritual of its own; it had a hierarchical form. A brotherhood of holy pastors, with mitre and crosier, and uplifted hand, walked forth and blessed and ruled a joyful people. The crucifix headed the procession, and simple monks were there with hearts in prayer, and sweet chants resounded, and the holy Latin tongue was heard, and boys came forth in white, swinging censers, and the fragrant cloud arose, and mass was sung, and the saints were invoked; and day after day, and in the still night, and over the woody hills and in the quiet plains, as constantly as sun, and moon and stars go forth in heaven, so regular and solemn was the stately march of blessed services of earth, high festival, and gorgeous procession, and soothing dirge, and passing bell, and the familiar evening call to prayer; till he who recollected the old pagan time would think it all unreal that he beheld and heard, and would conclude he did but see a vision, so marvellously was heaven let down upon earth, so triumphantly were chased away the fiends of darkness to their prison below.[3]

As Christianity spread, along with the expansion of the Roman Empire into pagan lands, and as the Empire itself was overrun by co-called 'barbarians' in successive waves of migration from the north, it could not successfully resist the influence of paganism on its worship. Pagan practices connected to spring festivals, for example, entered into the Christian observation of Easter. But are these examples of the Church being "polluted" by pagan elements, or are they signs of the Church's triumph over paganism, taking pagan symbols and investing them with Christian significance, thus triumphing over them? Debate continues over this important question but it is worth noting that the tendency of the Church to reflect its host culture in both positive and negative ways is not a phenomenon confined to the medieval period.

Some Features of Medieval Worship

In the twelfth century the invention of the "flying buttress" led to the construction of Gothic style cathedrals with tall spires and arches rising to previously impossible heights. The buttresses enabled a distribution of weight

---

3   John Henry Newman, in Fisher, 236-7.

to enable much higher structures, replacing the older basilica style. Left and right wings were added to the basilica pattern to provide more room, and to form the shape of a cross. The soaring architecture of the great cathedrals drew the worshipper's attention upward to the heavens, an effect still felt by those who enter them today. Cathedral construction could be the work of several generations, providing employment for the entire town and an opportunity for a profoundly communal expression of devotion.

The precise number of the sacraments was finally decided upon when the Council of Florence, in 1439, fixed them at seven in number. (Augustine, in the fifth century, had referred to up to thirty things as sacraments!) Peter Lombard listed the sacraments as seven in number in his *Sentences*, a medieval textbook for theological students, which was still being recommended for use during the sixteenth century Reformation period. The emphasis in thinking on the sacraments was not so much on their function as signs (though this idea remained) but much more on their function as *vehicles* of grace. The doctrine of "transubstantiation" based on Aristotle's distinction between "substance" and "accidence," was declared an official dogma, by Pope Innocent III, in 1215. The elements of bread and wine were said to be "changed" during the Mass, so that the "accidents" (bread and wine) remained the same, but the "essence" was transformed into the body and blood of Christ. In cathedral services, a bell would ring to announce the miracle of transformation for the benefit of those in the more remote parts of the building. Children were banned from participation in the Mass, lest the elements be spilled. Eventually the cup was withheld from the laity for the same reason. Thomas Aquinas developed the doctrine of "concomitance," in part to justify this practice. It stated that the bread was "accompanied by" the blood, as well as by the body, of Christ, so there was no need for the faithful to receive both of the elements. Roman Catholic churches today, influenced by the modernising impact of the Second Vatican Council (1962-1965), no longer insist on withholding the cup from the laity, though more conservative churches continue to do so.

The Latin Mass was at the heart of worship in the Western Church during the medieval period. The word "mass" comes from the Latin word for "dismissal" from the time when the catechumens were dismissed from the service before the baptised took Communion. In the medieval period there were several types of mass in use in the West and tracing its historical development is very difficult. The Low Mass (*Missa Lecta*) was spoken, and a cut-down version of the Sung Mass (*Missa Cantata*) became the main Sunday mass in a parish church. Few medieval Christians would ever have seen the High Mass performed; they participated only in what may have been offered in their town or village setting. In the later Middle Ages the private form of the Low Mass (without the choir and assistants required by the High Mass) became the standard way that the Mass was performed. The Roman Missal of the Counter Reformation period presented the private Mass as the standard form and the High Mass was consigned to very special occasions.[4]

If there is a fault in medieval worship it is that the Mass virtually eclipsed preaching and teaching, which were given a secondary, almost non-existent, role in the liturgy. Some objected to this trend. The Dominican, Humbert de Romanis, said that Christ celebrated the Mass only once (referring to the institution of the Lord's Supper), but spent his whole life preaching. Interestingly, the great philosophical theologian, Thomas Aquinas, though he wrote in Latin, preached to the people in the "vulgar" tongue – Italian.

An often forgotten element of medieval worship is the use of religious drama. The old pagan dramas had been stamped out and been replaced by "Mystery Plays" and "Miracle Plays" which focused on themes such as the creation, Jesus' life and passion, and the exploits of the apostles. These were at first composed and performed by the clergy, the church building serving as the performance space. They could be quite funny as well as very solemn depending on the focus of the story. Sadly such plays were excluded from the church by Pope Innocent III in 1210. Drama was then taken over by the secular performance artists, who began to satirise the church and its clergy. Eventually, in England, this art form would develop into the Elizabethan dramatic art of Shakespeare. Perhaps a lesson to be drawn here is that when the church boycotts a particular art form (such as television and cinema in our own time) it is often taken over by secular and "demonic" forces and used *against* the church and its message.

The Iconoclastic Controversy

One of the greatest "worship wars" to shake the early medieval church was the Iconoclastic Controversy of the eight century. Leo III (717-740) outlawed the use of icons (two-dimensional images of Christ and the saints used in worship) in 725. He wanted to purify the church from what he saw as "superstition" and he also had a political motive. He wanted a united empire and icons were offensive to Jews and Moslems alike, as well as to Gnostic sects, such as the Manichaens and the Paulicians, who idealised the "spirituality" of religion. The Hellenistic Christian sect of "Origenism" stressed "the intellectual and spiritual world of pure spirit…The image [it was believed] stands in the way of, rather than being a ladder to, that world."[5]

---

4   Bard Thompson, *Liturgies of the Western Church* (Philadelphia: Fortress Press, 1980), 45.

5   Fisher, 155-81.

The iconoclasts objected to icons on the following grounds:

1. The second commandment forbade graven images.
2. Humanity alone bears the image of God.
3. To portray a human visage of Christ separates his human nature from his divine nature or is a misplaced attempt to describe the divine in a limited way.

Those who argued for icons replied:

1. We do not venerate the icons, but those they depict.
2. Honour addressed to the saints is relative and not an absolute worship.
3. Icons are a necessary consequence of the invocation of saints.
4. If we ascribe value to relics, why not to icons?
5. The second commandment was only a temporary piece of legislation.
6. Icons are a help to devotion and are in universal use.[6]

A key to the argument in support of icons was the important distinction between "worship" and "veneration." The faithful may worship only God, but icons may rightly be venerated. The greatest theologian of the age, John of Damascus, whose *Fountain of Knowledge* is a complete systematic theology of eighth century Eastern Orthodoxy, contributed significantly to the debate over icons speaking persuasively in their defence. His views influenced the decision of the General Council in Nicaea in 787. This Council, considered by Orthodox Christians to be the last recognised ecumenical council was convened by Constantine VI, whose mother was a staunch "patron of pictures." The Council asserted that icons:

> 'should be given due salutation and honourable reverence, not indeed that true worship which pertains alone to the divine nature…For the honour which is paid to the image passes on to that which the image represents, and he who shows reverence to the image shows reverence to the subject represented in it.' Hence there triumphed the principle that the divine is not remote from the material world; but as in the Incarnation, the latter can be the medium of access to God.[7]

Of course, in the Incarnation itself we see the finest example of this principle, for God took on human flesh in the person of Jesus Christ, the "icon" of the

---

6 This summary is based on that given in Henry Chadwick, *The Early Church* (London: Penguin, 1993), 282.

7 Williston Walker, *A History of the Christian Church* (New York: Charles Scribner's Sons, 1959), 149.

invisible God. In entering into the world of matter God has made possible the holiness of material things.[8]

Before this principle was formally established however the Church was widely disrupted. Both monks and ordinary people revolted against the ban on icons. Leo III sent out military troops to enforce his decree. Back in Rome, a Synod was called in 731, under Pope Gregory III, which asserted the validity of images and excommunicated all opponents of icons. Leo's successor, his son Constantine V, pursued his father's policy even more vigorously. At a Synod in Constantinople in 754, images were again condemned because they were thought to lower the worshippers' adoration from the world of spirit to the material realm. In this controversy, the papacy tore itself away from Eastern emperors and the already-existing gap between East and West was significantly widened.

Music in the Medieval Period

We have seen that while the Low Mass was spoken, it was a reduced version of the Sung Mass that became the main Sunday mass in a parish church. The High Mass or Festival Mass (*Missa Solemnis*) was sung on special occasions, often with a large choir. While the Roman Mass limited singing to the clergy, a much greater congregational participation was evident in the German Church of the Middle Ages. Many melodies of popular origin were sung during penitential processions and pilgrimages.[9] The Scandinavian regions were evangelised primarily by the German Church, and also gave rise to some wonderful sung music.

There are five great prayers in the Mass - the *Kyrie* ("Lord have mercy..."), the *Gloria in excelsis Deo* ("Glory to God in the highest..."); the *Credo* ("I believe..."; the *Sanctus et Benedictus* ("Holy, holy, holy...") and the *Agnus Dei* "lamb of God..."). These five prayers have been put to music by such great masters as Palestrina, Bach, Haydn, Mozart, Beethoven, and Stravinsky. We have noted that the Eastern Liturgy remained non-instrumental up to the present day. Basic organs began to appear in the West in the eighth century. By the twelfth century their use in the Mass was common. At first, the organ was used to set the pitch for unaccompanied chants and choral parts. It then developed a repertoire of its own, playing responses to portions of the sung Mass, and finally became a solo instrument in its own right.

---

8 Iconographers stress the importance of the natural materials used in writing icons, including eggs and vegetable and mineral dyes. Combined with prayer, fasting, and the Word these materials come to share in the holy.

9 See Hustad, *Jubilate II*, 181.

This was also a flowering age of religious verse, much of which was turned into hymnody. Among the medieval hymns that have survived in use today, some of the most commonly found are those of Bernard of Clairveaux, such as *Jesu the Joy of Loving Hearts*, *Jesus, the Very Thought of You*, and *O Sacred Head Once Wounded*. Francis of Assisi (1182-1226) wrote many vernacular hymns of praise called *laude*, influenced by the style of the French troubadours. Later these developed into more complex songs using folk song tunes and dance melodies. German *Geisslerieder* and *Leisen* were crusading or pilgrim songs, sung in processional litanies in the fourteenth century. The visionary mystic, Hildegard of Bingen (1098-1197) used extended melody lines based on earlier chants, and developed some of the earliest written musical notation. Exposure to the Middle Eastern Islamic culture, as a result of the Crusades, is also reflected in the musical styles of the medieval period.

Giovanni da Palestrina (c. 1525-1594) was a great Italian composer whose polyphonic music is some of the most complex ever written. The *Missa Papae Marcelli* is one of his most famous masses. Composed in 1567 it was "described as a totally new style."[10] William Byrd (1543-1623), writing during the Reformation (late medieval) period, wrote music for the Catholic Mass as well as for the reformed Anglican rite.

Summary

The medieval Mass was a solemn drama with considerable power over the imaginations of the worshippers, but it had the weakness of being almost entirely an act of clergy observed passively by a spectator congregation in a language (Latin) often unknown to them. A very high view of the sacrament of the Eucharist, a stress on the divinity of Christ, sometimes at the expense of his humanity, the use of incense, icons, candles, robed clergy and the construction of impressive cathedrals all contributed to a note of transcendence in worship. The attention of worshippers was drawn upwards into heaven, away from this material world of death and decay to the undying world of life, light, and holiness. However, literacy levels were often quite poor, even among the clergy, so worship suffered from a continuation of historic practices that were not rigorously subjected to the text of Scripture. The Reformation period, beginning with Martin Luther's calls for reform in 1517, would see the church's worship radically altered by an appeal to the Scriptures as the final authority on patterns of worship.

Some Questions

1. Modern people sometimes have a rather dim view of the Middle Ages

---

10   Liner notes, *An Introduction to Early Music* (Naxos CD, 1995), 15.

as a backward and superstitious era. What are some of the positive things about the church's worship at this time that might counteract such a negative view?

2. Do you see the appropriation of pagan symbols and ideas into Christianity as a sign of the corruption of the Church or as a sign of its triumph over paganism?

3. If you have ever worshipped in a cathedral take some time to now to reflect on (or discuss) your experience. What drew your attention and what affect did the space have on your senses?

4. Do you believe that the use of images in worship is appropriate? Does it aid worship or only distract from it?

For Further Reading

Senn, Frank C. *Christian Liturgy: Catholic and Evangelical.* Minneapolis, MN: Fortress Press, 1997.

Thompson, Bard. *Liturgies of the Western Church.* Philadelphia: Fortress Press, 1961.

Wegman, Herman. *Christian Worship in East and West: A Study Guide to Christian Liturgy.* New York: Peublo, 1985.

White, James F. *Documents of Christian Worship: Descriptive and Interpretive Sources.* Louisville: Westminster/John Knox Press, 1992.

You can read an English translation of the Latin Mass at the *Medieval Source-Book* site: http://www.fordham.edu/halsall/basis/latinmass2.html

CHAPTER SIX

Worship in the Reformation: From Temple to Auditorium

The Protestant Reformation was a sixteenth century movement that sought to return to the Bible as the authority for Christian life, theology, and worship, rather than to depend upon the authority of the Church, and of the papacy. Though all the Reformers agreed that the Bible was to have the final say, they did not all agree about *the way* the Bible should function authoritatively in the church's worship. An example of this is the contrasting views of Martin Luther and John Calvin. According to Luther, only what is expressly *condemned* in scripture should be excluded from worship. If the Bible has nothing to say about it one way or the other, then it's okay to use it. Calvin, on the other hand maintained that only what is expressly *commended* in scripture, and in particular in the New Testament, should be included in worship. We should not have anything in worship, says Calvin, for which we do not have an explicit biblical reference. For example, Luther had no problem with instrumental music in worship, since the New Testament does not prohibit it. Calvin, on the other hand banned instrumental worship in church because there was no direct reference to it in the New Testament.

Lutheran Worship

Martin Luther (1483-1546) defined the Church as that company of people wherein the Word of God is rightly preached and the sacraments rightly administered. Worship, therefore, was essentially a matter of Word and Table in the centre of the baptised community. He was quite critical of the worship practices of his time. "There is today in the churches, a great ringing of bells, blowing of trumpets, singing, shouting, and intoning, yet I fear precious little worship of God…[T]o think to worship God with many words and a great noise is to count Him either deaf or ignorant, and to suppose we must waken or instruct Him. Such an opinion of God tends to His shame and dishonour rather than to His worship."[1] The devil would fear a "pig-sty" where prayer was truly offered more than all the "high and beautiful churches, towers and bells in existence, if such prayer be not in them."[2]

At first, Luther simply used a shortened version of the Roman Mass. In his first liturgy, *Formula missae et communionis* (1523), hymns, scripture readings,

---

1   Hugh T. Kerr, ed. *A Compend of Luther's Theology* (Philadelphia: Westminster, 1974), 144.
2   Kerr, 145-6

and sermon were to be in German; Latin was retained for the rest. His later German Mass, the *Deutsche messe* (1526), was more radical. The whole of the service is in the vernacular (German), though the Greek of the *Kyrie eleison* is retained. Both of Luther's masses were used in Lutheran churches. The more formal *Formula missae* tended to be used in cathedral and college settings, and the *Deutsche messe* in smaller towns and villages.

According to Luther, the worship of God is two-fold. It has both outward and inward components and it arises out of the experience of God's grace.[3] Variations in the liturgy are quite acceptable; each one should be convinced in his or her own mind and give liberty to others. After all, it is not external rites that commend us to God but faith and love.

> Even if different people make use of different rites, let no one either judge or despise the other; but let each one abound in his own opinion, and let them understand and know even if they do differently; and let each one's rite be agreeable to the other, lest diverse opinions and sects yield diverse uses, just as happened in the Roman Church. For external rites, even if we are not able to do without them - just as we cannot do without food and drink - nevertheless, do not commend us to God, just as food and drink does not commend us to God. Wherefore, let this word of Paul govern here: The kingdom of God is not food and drink, but righteousness, peace, and joy in the Holy Spirit. Thus no rite is the Kingdom of God, but faith within you, etc.[4]

Luther was keen to eliminate the overcrowding of the Christian calendar with saints days.[5] Instead of such days being used for devout exercises they tended to be used in "loafing, gluttony, and drunkenness, gambling and other evil deeds; and then the mass and the sermon are listened to without edification, the prayer is spoken without faith...It is all so formal and superficial!"[6] Ceremonies were compared by Luther to the models and plans of builders. They are important, but they are not the actual building. If a builder spent all of his life admiring his plans and drawings and models, and never got around to building anything, would we not think him crazy? Yet some approach worship in this manner.[7]

---

3   Martin Luther, *Table Talk* (London: Harper Collins, 1995), 78.

4   Martin Luther, "Formula of Mass and Communion for the Church at Wittenberg," *Works of Martin Luther, Vol. VI.* 92f, cited in Kerr, 142-3.

5   For a contemporary reappropriation of the commemoration of saints into the Protestant calendar see Robert Gribben, "Saints under the Southern Cross: The Uniting Church in Australia," Stephen Burns and Anita Monro, eds. *Christian Worship in Australia: Inculturating the Liturgical Tradition* (Sydney: St. Paul's, 2009), 91-105.

6   Martin Luther, "Treatise on Good Works," *Works of Martin Luther, Vol. I.*, 222, cited in Kerr, 143.

7   Luther, "Treatise on Good Works," 347, cited in Kerr, 143-4.

Luther did not see himself as abolishing the whole of medieval worship and starting from scratch. He was not a liturgical "restorationist" or iconoclast, but saw himself as standing within the Catholic liturgical tradition. Unlike the later English Puritans, it was not his wish to "demolish idols" and begin again, but to purify that order of worship which was currently in use.

> It is not now, nor has it ever been, in our mind to abolish entirely the whole formal cultus of God, but to cleanse that which is in use, which has been vitiated [that is, corrupted and debased, made weak and ineffective] by most abominable additions, and to point out a pious use. For this cannot be denied, that masses and the communion of bread and wine are a rite divinely instituted by Christ, which was observed, first under Christ Himself, then under the apostles, most simply, and piously without any additions. But so many human inventions have been added to it in due course of time, that nothing of the mass and communion has come down to our age except the name.[8]

The Augsburg Confession (1539) penned by Luther's lieutenant Philip Melanchthon (1497-1560), was the first formal statement of the Lutheran confessional tradition. A number of the Articles deal directly with worship. "Article VII: Of the Church" states that it is not necessary that "human traditions, that is, rites or ceremonies, instituted by men, should be everywhere alike." "Article XV: Of Ecclesiastical Usages" allows that some practices, such as the keeping of holy days can profitably be observed in the church without sin but makes it clear that "human traditions instituted to propitiate God, to merit grace, and to make satisfaction for sins, are opposed to the Gospel and the doctrine of faith. Wherefore vows and traditions concerning meats and days, etc., instituted to merit grace and to make satisfaction for sins, are useless and contrary to the Gospel."[9]

Reformed Worship

In addition to the Lutheran churches of the European Reformation there were also those churches who looked more to the leadership and theology of the French reformer John Calvin (1509-1564) for their inspiration. These are referred to as "Reformed" or "Presbyterian" churches. A young humanist scholar and a student of law, Calvin was converted to Protestant views while

---

8   Martin Luther, "Formula of Mass and Communion for the Church at Wittenberg," *Works of Martin Luther, Vol. VI.*, 84ff, cited in Kerr, 144.

9   *The Confession of Faith: Which Was Submitted to His Imperial Majesty Charles V At the Diet of Augsburg in the Year 1530 by Philip Melanchthon, 1497-1560.* Translated by F. Bente and W. H. T. Dau, in *Triglot Concordia: The Symbolical Books of the Evangelical Lutheran Church* (St. Louis: Concordia, 1921), 37-95. The text of the confession is available online at http://www.ctsfw.edu/etext/boc/ac/ accessed 30 April 2013.

undertaking his studies. He had decided to devote himself entirely to study, but upon visiting the Swiss city of Geneva, the reformer William Farel persuaded him, after much effort, to stay and organise a Protestant reformation there. In 1537 all of the townspeople were called upon to swear loyalty to a Protestant statement of faith. When Calvin first preached at Geneva he seems not to have followed any set liturgy at all, and there was no instrumental music.

During his time as a pastor in Strasbourg Calvin borrowed from Martin Bucer's German rite to create his French liturgy of 1540. This was simplified in Geneva becoming the widely used "Geneva rite," a liturgy that came into standard use among the Reformed churches on the Continent. Calvin was convinced that some kind of order in worship must be prescribed, but insisted that nothing was to be allowed in public worship that could not be drawn from scripture. He eliminated "Roman" elements and all prayers to Mary and to the saints. The place of the sermon was exalted to a very high place.

Pure religion, according to Calvin, was a uniting of faith and fear, hence the rather solemn and reverential nature of Presbyterian and Reformed worship to this day. Fear mingled with faith produces "a voluntary reverence...[and] legitimate worship agreeable to the injunctions of the law...[M]en in general render to God a formal worship, but very few truly reverence him; while great ostentation in ceremonies is universally displayed, but sincerity of heart is rarely to be found."[10]

The Reformed approach to worship was most consistently followed by the Puritans of the seventeenth century.[11] The Church of England generally followed Luther's "permissive" rule. But the Puritan party within the Church favoured Calvin's "restrictive" rule. Both parties agreed on the authority of Scripture, but they differed on how to *apply* the Scripture to worship. The inability to resolve such disputes was one contributing factor to the eventual formation of Presbyterian and Independent churches thus giving birth to the Nonconformist tradition in English religious life. Calvin had said that the *Book of Common Prayer* (discussed in a later section of this chapter) contained "many tolerable pieces of foolishness." The Puritans agreed, and specifically wanted to remove such things as the surplice (the white linen garment worn by the priest),[12] wedding rings, using the sign of the cross in baptism, and kneeling at Holy Communion. All ceremonies, they argued, must have direct

---

10   Hugh Kerr, ed. *A Compend of the Institutes of the Christian Religion by John Calvin* (London: Lutterworth Press, 1965), 6.
11   Material for this section is drawn largely from James I. Packer. *A Quest for Godliness: The Puritan Vision of the Christian Life* (Wheaton: Crossways Books, 1990), 245-57.
12   The surplice is a cut-down alb with large sleeves to be worn over warmer clothes in the cold Northern European climate.

biblical warrant or they are wrong. John Owen, at one time Vice Chancellor of Oxford University, represents the Puritan position well when he states, "God's worship hath no accidentals…all that is in it and belonging to it, and the manner of it, is false worship, if it have not a divine institution in particular."[13]

This position was contrary to the Anglican Article XXXIV, "Of the Traditions of the Church" which states that "It is not necessary that traditions and ceremonies be in all places one or utterly alike; for at all times they have been diverse, and may be changed according to the diversity of countries, times, and men's manners, so that nothing be ordained against God's word…every particular or national Church hath authority to ordain, change, and abolish ceremonies or rites of the Church ordained only by man's authority, so that [i.e. "so long as"] all things be done to edifying."[14] Owen accused the "imposers of liturgies" of bringing "Fire and faggot [that is, persecution] into the Christian religion…Liturgies and set forms must be abandoned like crutches that God's people may walk in the power of faith."[15] The Congregationalist party among the English Puritans persuaded their Presbyterian colleagues to drop their call for a Geneva-based liturgy, in favour of the *Directory for the Public Worship of God throughout the Three Kingdoms* (1644).

The Puritans used some rather remarkable proof-texts to defend their own unique practices. Numbers 28:9 ("On the sabbath day [make an offering of] two male lambs a year old without blemish…") they took as proof that there should be two Sunday services; 2 Timothy 1:13 made the use of a catechism obligatory ("Hold to the standard of sound teaching that you have heard from me…"); Romans 8:26 proved set liturgies to be unlawful ("Likewise, the Spirit helps us in our weakness; for we do not know how to pray as we ought but that very Spirit intercedes with sighs too deep for words"); Acts 1:15 proved that the minister should remain standing in one place during the service ("In those days Peter stood up among the believers…"); and 1 Corinthians 14:31 was used to justify the Puritan practice of area-wide "prophesyings," that is, protracted preaching meetings that were carried out outside the Anglican parochial system ("For you can all prophesy in turn so that all may learn and all be encouraged.") These verses do not in fact prove the points being made;

---

13   Cited by James Packer in "The Puritan Approach to Worship," http://www.the-highway.com/Puritan-worship_Packer.html, accessed 30 April 2013.
14   Article XXXIV, "Of the Traditions of the Church," *The Book of Common Prayer* (London: Folio Society, 2004), 713.
15   Horton Davies, "Congregationalist Worship," in J.G. Davies, ed. *The New Westminster Dictionary of Liturgy and Worship* (Philadelphia: Westminster Press, 1986), 191-92.

at best they are *suggestive* of such practices. This only goes to prove that the phrase, "It's biblical," often means little more than, "That's the way I see it"!

In seventeenth century England there were three possibilities for regulating worship. Either one used the set liturgy of the Anglican *Book of Common Prayer*, or the Presbyterian manual of general guidance, *The Westminster Directory*, or individual ministers and congregations would be left to their own devices to develop patterns of their own as became the practice among Independents, Quakers, and Baptists. The only clearly sanctioned pattern, legally speaking, remained the Prayer Book, and from 1662 Anglican ministers could be thrown out of their parishes (ejected) if they did not use it, as were both of John Wesley's grandfathers John Benjamin Wesley and Samuel Annesley, in addition to his great-grandfather Bartholomew Westley, in the Great Ejection of that year.[16]

To pursue strict conformity in worship to the point of applying legal penalties such as imprisonment and even death for breach of that conformity seems futile and would certainly be impossible today. Yet some discipline does seem necessary. How can churches ensure that the extremes of hyper-Pentecostal behaviours such as those associated with the so-called "Toronto Blessing" (laughing uncontrollably, spinning around on the spot, and barking like a dog, for example) are kept out of its liturgy? And what of extreme liberal liturgical texts which do not sufficiently reflect the received faith of the church? Liturgical innovations such as the replacement of wine and bread in the Eucharist with milk and honey may seem to go too far for many. Even if it might be argued that there is a precedent for the use of milk and honey in the Old Testament and in Hippolytus, what about the suggestion that beer and pretzels, or coke and burgers, should replace bread and wine, because they might in some contexts be more culturally appropriate? There is a need for some kind of standard to be applied to worship but how to do so in a culture that favours innovation and independence of action is difficult to determine. While the legal penalties of the seventeenth century may seem extreme, today's "anything goes" policy creates its own set of problems.

The Puritans defined worship as "doxology," that is, rendering glory to God. All true piety was a form of worship, which took place in the three spheres of the local church (public), the family circle (domestic) and in the prayer closet (private). The Puritans believed that every home should be a "little church," with the father, as head of the house, playing the role of the minister. Twice daily, families were

---

16   Kenneth J. Collins, *A Real Christian: The Life of John Wesley* (Nashville: Abingdon Press, 1999), 9.

to hear the Word read, and join in prayer. Interestingly, public worship was considered the most exalted type, because it was closest to that worship which is offered in heaven. Simplicity was designed as the safeguard of inwardness and the Scriptures were the safeguard of truth. Puritans are sometimes criticized for their rather sombre and austere approach to worship, but to them such worship was a thing of beauty. Elements of Puritan worship included:

1. Praise (metrical versions of the Psalms only)
2. Prayer (confession, adoration, intercession)
3. Preaching (considered the most crucial test of a person's ministry and the high point of the liturgy)
4. Sacraments (or "Ordinances")
5. Catechising.
6. Church discipline.

The Puritans believed in *preparing* the heart for worship. One Puritan wrote, "If thou wouldst…leave thy heart with God on Saturday night, thou shouldst find it with him in the Lord's Day morning."[17] Some have argued that we do not need new liturgies, new hymns, new tunes, or new styles of worship, so much as we need more "heart-work" to prepare for those we already have. Without this, we will only suffer from more of what C. S. Lewis called "the liturgical fidgets."

Quaker Worship

The Religious Society of Friends (whose members are popularly known as "Quakers") emerged out of the life and experience of George Fox (1624-91) during the tumultuous period of the English Civil War. Their doctrine of an "Inner Light" saw God as working directly upon the soul bringing a sense of communion with the divine independent of Scripture, Church and Creed. Quaker meetings are often characterised by silence as members (there are no clergy) sit together in the presence of God and await the Spirit's inner movement upon the hearts of those gathered. Spoken utterances are only brought to the gathering if the Spirit so moves. There is no sacramental observance as such, except in the sense that all of life is seen as having a sacramental quality. The New Testament practices of Baptism and Eucharist are seen as belonging to a kind of transitionary period between the Old Testament age of rituals and the New Testament age of the Spirit. Now that the Spirit has come in fullness there is thought to be no further need for rituals of any kind.

---

17   George Swinnock, *Works* (Edinburgh: James Nichol, 1868) Vol. I, p. 31.

Quakers were convinced that no mere external rite can produce spiritual change in a person. Water baptism merely diverts attention from the baptism of the Spirit. As for the Lord's command to "Do this in remembrance of me," Quakers saw ordinary meal times taken with thanksgiving as fulfilling this instruction. They saw the limitation of sacramental observance to clergy, whether Catholic or Protestant, as placing a limitation on the priesthood of all believers. The "offices" of Christ as prophet, priest, and king were to be responded to "in silent, attentive, and expectant waiting."[18]

The 1675 Confession of the Society of Friends defined baptism in a radically "spiritual" way.

> As there is one Lord and one faith, so there is "one baptism; which is not the putting away the filth of the flesh, but the answer of a good conscience before God, by the resurrection of Jesus Christ." And this baptism is a pure and spiritual thing, to wit, the baptism of the Spirit and fire...of which the baptism of John was a figure, which was commanded for a time, and not to be continued forever.[19]

Similarly, "the communion of the body and blood of Christ is inward and spiritual, which is the participation of his flesh and blood, by which the inward man is daily nourished in the hearts of those in whom Christ dwells." The breaking of bread by Christ with his disciples was equated with other "figures" such as 'abstaining from things strangled and from blood'; the washing one another's feet, and the anointing of the sick with oil;...seeing they are but the shadow of better things, they cease in such as have obtained the substance."[20]

Anglican Worship

The *Thirty Nine Articles* state the position of the Church of England on a number of matters pertinent to our study. "Article XX Of the Authority of the Church" states that

> The Church hath power to decree rites or ceremonies and authority in controversies of faith; and yet it is not lawful for the Church to ordain anything contrary to God's word written, neither may it so expound one place of Scripture, that it be repugnant to another. Wherefore, although

---

18   M.A. Creasey, "Quaker Worship," in J.G. Davies, *Westminster Dictionary of Liturgy*, 454-55.

19   "The Confession of the Society of Friends, Commonly Called Quakers (1675)," 12th Proposition, "Concerning Baptism," in Philip Schaff, ed. *The Creeds of Christendom, with Historical and Critical Notes. Volume III: The Evangelical Protestant Creeds with Translation* (New York: Harper and Brothers, 1877), 797.

20   13th Proposition, "Concerning the Communion, or Participation of the Body and Blood of Christ," in Schaff, *Creeds of Christendom*, III: 797.

the Church be a witness and a keeper of Holy Writ: yet, as it ought not to decree anything against the same, so besides the same ought it not to enforce anything to be believed for necessity of salvation.[21]

Here we see the typically Protestant insistence that all matters, including worship, should be determined on the basis of Holy Scripture. Yet Anglican worship has also been profoundly shaped by its pre-Reformation Catholic heritage. Nowhere is the struggle and synthesis between these two traditions clearer than in the development of *The Book of Common Prayer*.

Henry VIII, who is usually credited with beginning the Reformation in England, was certainly no friend to Protestantism. He wrote against Luther's ideas and was given the title, by the Pope, of "Defender of the Faith," before he had his final falling out with Rome. Wanting an annulment of his marriage to Catherine of Aragon which the Pope refused to give, Henry turned to the Archbishop of Canterbury Thomas Cranmer (1489-1556), who held more Protestant views, and took the opportunity to establish a Lutheran style reform in England (Later, Calvin's influence would also be felt). This was not what Henry had anticipated; his preference was essentially that there should be an English Catholic Church with himself instead of the Pope as Head. Cranmer replaced the Latin Mass with the English Prayer Book with the approval and enforcement of Parliament. His 1549 *Book of Common Prayer* underwent subsequent revisions in 1552, influenced by the *Censura* composed by the Swiss Refomer Martin Bucer. The 1662 edition remains authoritative in the Anglican Communion.

Cranmer drew on several earlier works in the development of the first English Prayer Book. The Spanish Cardinal Quinonez, General of the Franciscans, produced his *Reformed Breviary*, which enjoyed the approval of the pope for thirty years. First published in 1535, and revised in 1537, it was designed for the use of the monastic "hours" of prayer among the clergy. It simplified the Offices, discarding medieval overlays, restricted readings from the saints' lives, and focused on the uninterrupted reading of Scripture. It formed, in part, the basis for Cranmer's revision of the *Sarum Breviary*, which eventually became the Anglican Order for Morning and Evening Prayer. This was an attempt to give not only to the clergy, but to the whole people of God, the opportunity of a daily discipline of the "hours" for use in the secular life. Much of the Preface to the First Edwardian Prayer Book of 1549 was a literal translation from Quinonez's work.

---

21   Article XX, "Of the Authority of the Church," *The Book of Common Prayer* (London: Folio Society, 2004), 709.

In 1543 a royal order was given to the effect that one chapter of the English Bible should be read in every parish church each Sunday and holy day after the *Te Deum* and the *Magnificat*. An *English Litany* was produced in 1544, to be used in processions, which purged the medieval Litany of its invocation of saints. These very few revisions were almost the full extent of the liturgical reforms to take place under Henry, who never warmed toward Protestant innovations. Cranmer remained at work behind the scenes, drawing together in an unofficial capacity, several drafts of large scale liturgical reforms.

In 1547, the first year of the reign of the boy king Edward VI, the Royal Injunctions ordered that the Epistle and Gospel at High Mass should be read in English. The first Book of Homilies was also published. An Act of Parliament in 1548 restored Communion in both kinds and an Order of Communion was prepared in March of that year to enable the churches to carry out that Act. The work for this first Edwardian Prayer Book was assigned to a committee which met first at Cranmer's country house at Chertsey and then later at Windsor. We have no official listing of the names of the bishops and "learned men" who made up the committee, but clearly Cranmer was its guiding architect.[22] Upon completion the new *Prayer Book* was authorized and enjoined upon the public by way of the first *Act of Uniformity*, which was passed on 21 January 1549. This first *Prayer Book* was not universally received with gratitude. A local rebellion took place in the West of England, complaining that the new service book was "like a Christmas game." The crown responded by pointing out that what seemed to be new and innovative, was nothing other than the old faith freed from its medieval obscurity by bringing it into the vernacular. Of course, this was something of an understatement, as it was in fact the beginning of the radical Protestantising of the English Church which would be the cause of so much civil and ecclesiastical conflict over the next several decades.

Cranmer came under increasing pressure from more radically Protestant figures such as the continentals John a Lasco, and Peter Martyr, and the English Bishops Ridley and Hooper, to revise the *Prayer Book*. These felt that the liturgy had made too many concessions to Rome. The extent to which the pressure of this more radical element was applied to Cranmer, and how much affect it had on the revised Prayer Book of 1552 is hotly contested. The later nineteenth century Anglo-Catholic movement wanted to portray Cranmer as a good Catholic who was bullied into revision by the "Puritan" party. Evangelicals, on the other hand, were less willing to concede this and portrayed Cranmer as a man whose mind was decidely made up in terms

---

22   The details of the Committee's work are tragically lost to us, however, as the records of Convocation for that year were lost in the great fire of London in 1666.

the Continental Reformers favoured. In any cases major changes were made in the new book which do seem to be the result of Continental influences, both Calvinist and Zwinglian. While the printing process was under way, the work was called to a halt in September of 1552, in an attempt to remove the requirement to kneel at the Holy Communion. Cranmer, however, would not yield on this point, and referred to the more scrupulous Protestants as "those glorious and unquiet spirits which can like nothing but that is after their own fancy, and cease not to make trouble and disquietness when things are most quiet and in good order. If such men should be heard, although the Book were made every year anew, yet should it not lack faults in their opinion."[23]

He responds to the standard Reformed position that "whatsoever is not commanded in the Scriptures is against the Scripture, and utterly unlawful and ungodly" as follows.

> But this saying is the chief foundation of the error of the Anabaptists and of divers other sects. This saying is a subversion of all order as well in religion as in common polity. If this saying be true, take away the whole Book of Service...If the kneeling of the people should be discontinued for the time of receiving of the Sacrament, so that at the receipt thereof, they should rise up and stand or sit, and then immediately kneel down again, it should rather import a contemptuous than a reverent receiving of the Sacrament....[I]f we will follow the plain words of Scripture, we shall rather receive it lying down on the ground, as the custom of the world at that time [was] almost everywhere, as the Tartars and Turks use yet at this day.[24]

Contemporary liturgical renewal has focused on the need to recover very early sources, and to recapture the worship practices of the primitive church. This does not seem to have been Cranmer's approach. His library, his Parliamentary debate on the 1549 Prayer Book, and his controversial writings all give evidence that he was familiar with such sources. He knew the liturgical relevance of Justin Martyr, Tertullian, Cyprian, pseudo-Dionysius, Isidore, Chrysostom, the Mozarabic Missal, and the epiclesis from the Eastern liturgies. He was also extremely well read in Eucharistic theology. His primary concern however was to recover a biblical theology of worship and to have this reflected in the liturgy.

---

23   Bishop Gibson, Introduction, *The First and Second Prayer Books of Edward VI.* (London: J.M. Dent and Sons and New York: E.P. Dutton, 1949), xiv.

24   Cited in Henry Gee, *The Elizabethan Prayer Book and Ornaments* (London: Macmillan and Co., 1902), 225-226.

Cranmer accepted the principle that the shape of the liturgy must be determined not by the medieval Mass, nor by the Eastern services with which he was acquainted but by the words of Scripture. He was always one to go back to origins. With extraordinary skill he brought together all that could be gleaned from the New Testament about the way in which the Eucharist is to be understood, at the same time retaining all that seemed to him to be truly scriptural from the great liturgical tradition of the west. Hence the Passover atmosphere of the 1552 liturgy, and the eschatological elements, which are present, though not over-stressed. Once this is grasped, the shape begins to take shape; the service is not a random collection of fragments, but a great symphonic movement, unbroken from "Lift up your hearts" to the blessing.[25]

The new book came into use on All Saints Day, November 1st 1552. Its life, however, was a short one as Edward died in the summer of 1553, and Mary Tudor's ascension to the throne saw the restoration of the Latin Mass and the repeal of the second Act of Uniformity. The second Edwardian Prayer Book "marks the extreme limit to which the liturgical changes proceeded in England."[26] For the more Catholic-minded this meant "the low-water mark of Anglican liturgical usage and doctrinal expression."[27] With the restoration to Protestantism after a brief but fiery Marian reign, Elizabeth I and Archbishop Matthew Parker kept the forces of Puritanism and Catholicism at bay to come up with a 1559 revision which was something of a balance between the two earlier books. Of the 9,400 clergy called to subscribe to the 1559 Book only 189 refused to conform.

James I presided over a Conference of Puritans and Traditionalists at Hampton Court in 1604 which resulted in only minor changes. During Oliver Cromwell's Protectorate, the Presbyterians and Independents introduced the *Reformed Directory*, and the use of the earlier *Prayer Book* became illegal. Charles II finally reinstated it in a 1661 revision, after hearing the claims of Presbyterians and others at the Savoy Conference. It was now for the first time bound together with the Psalter. A Committee of Convocation, backed by an Act of Uniformity in 1662 finalised the basic shape of Anglican liturgy down to the present day. The final version carries the marks of the struggle between Catholic and Evangelical parties in the Church of England a struggle

25   Stephen Neill, "Liturgical Continuity and Change in the Anglican Churches," in David Martin and Peter Mullen, eds. *No Alternative: The Prayer Book Controversy* (Oxford: Basil Blackwell, 1981), 8-9.

26   Gibson, Introduction, vii-viii.

27   Stella Brook, *The Language of the Book of Common Prayer* (London: Andre Deutsch, 1965), 29, citing H.A.L. Rice.

which has brought something glorious out of the human weaknesses of the prolonged disputes. All subsequent "Alternative Services" have used this 1662 *Prayer Book* as their point of departure.

It is hard to overestimate the significance of Thomas Cranmer and his "immortal bequest" in the *Book of Common Prayer*. Not only in the worldwide Anglican Communion but in the worship rites of most branches of Methodism, and other Protestant churches, elements of the *Prayer Book* can be found. Perhaps no book, with the exception of the King James Version of the Bible, has done so much to shape the religious consciousness of the English-speaking world.

Music in the Reformation Period

Luther on Music

Martin Luther was himself a musician who loved both the music and the Latin text of the Mass. "I am not of the opinion," he wrote, "that all arts are to be cast down and destroyed on account of the Gospel, as some fanatics protest; on the other hand I would gladly see all arts, especially music, in the service of Him who has given and created them."[28] In 1530 he began to outline a treatise on music, which was never completed. Quoting Augustine he said, "For music is a gift...of God, not a gift of men...Therefore, accustom yourself to see in music your Creator and to praise him through it."[29] According to Luther, preachers should not be ordained without skills in music. "Music is a noble gift of God, next to theology. I would not change my little knowledge of music for a great deal."[30] Some musicologists, such as Victor Gebauer, believe Luther understood music to be "the language of God" and that the "power of music, used for good purpose, could produce the same effect as the Word of the Gospel."[31]

In Luther's liturgy directions were given for chants and modes. He also replaced historic Latin hymns with German metrical versions set to popular musical styles. He was indifferent, and at times hostile, to the use of organs in church. Beyond setting the tone for the unaccompanied singing he did not favour their use. This suspicion of the organ was also common among Catholics of the time. Luther himself wrote many excellent hymns, which have been retained in the use of most Protestant churches. He chose tunes from earlier worship modes (e.g. the *leisen* of the medieval pilgrims), or borrowed secular tunes. He borrowed the tune from the love song "Wake up, wake up,

---

28   Kerr, *Compend*, 146.
29   Hustad, 186.
30   Kerr, 147.
31   Victor Gebauer, "Theology of Church Music, Reformers," in Carl Schalk, ed. *Key Words in Church Music* (St. Louis: Concordia, 1978), 337-9.

you beauty" for "Dear Christians, one and all, rejoice." Lutherans after Luther's time did the same. For example the song "Innsbruck, I now must leave you," was altered to "O world, I now must leave you." Two of Luther's best-known hymns are paraphrases of Psalms - *A Mighty Fortress is Our God* (Psalm 46), and *Out of the Depths I Cry to You* (Psalm 130).

Calvin on Music

Endorsing only the congregational singing of metrical versions of the Psalms, Calvin favoured music in the home and in school life, but feared that its use in church would distract worshippers from more "spiritual" worship. The Scots particularly followed Calvin in restricting sung musical texts to Psalms and other scriptural passages. With the help of the French court poet Clement Marot, and Calvin's colleague Theodore Beza, all one hundred and fifty Psalms were set to metre in the Genevan Psalter of 1562. These were to be sung, in French, by the congregation with no musical accompaniment. The music editor of this work was Louis Bourgeois (c. 1510-1561) who adapted tunes from French and German secular songs and selections from Gregorian chant, as well as composing some of his own music in similar styles. These were very different from other church music of the time, their dance rhythms leading some to mock them as "Geneva jigs."

Music in the English Liturgy

John Merbecke (c. 1510-1585) set certain songs in the Book of Common Prayer to syllabic chants based on original melodies of his own, and some were adapted from Gregorian chants. These earlier settings were later abandoned as the church in England came under increasingly Calvinist influences. Myles Coverdale had made an English translation of German and Latin hymns in 1543 which he called *Goostly psalmes and spirituall songs*. These were for use in private chapels and homes, rather than in the Sunday liturgy. But again, this approach was frowned upon as the church came more and more under the influence of Calvin's thought with its preference for metrical psalms only.

At the end of the reign of Henry VIII, Thomas Sternhold produced a small book of nineteen metrical Psalms entitled *Groom of the Royal Wardrobe* (c.1547). His purpose was to provide for the young King Edward VI and his royal court a more spiritual substitute for the "trivial, secular court ballads."[32] Most of the early English Psalms were in "ballad metre" (8.6.8.6), later called "Common Metre," so they may also have been sung to popular ballad tunes. In 1549 a larger Psalter appeared with thirty-six psalms by Sternhold and a further eight by his collaborator John Hopkins.

---

32   Hustad, *Jubilate II*, 199.

When Mary Tudor ascended the throne, the country reverted to the earlier Roman rite and many Protestant leaders, known as "the Marian exiles," fled to the Continent. When they returned under Elizabeth I they brought with them a renewed interest in the Psalms. Based on Sternhold and Hopkins' earlier work, and influenced by Calvin's French Psalter, the entire book of Psalms soon appeared in English (in 1562) and this Sternhold and Hopkins collection would dominate English worship music for the next two hundred years. The English church followed Luther, rather than Calvin, however, when it came to the use of choirs. The choir both led the congregation and sang alone, especially in the cathedrals and royal chapels. Tudor composers who had earlier written Latin Masses, such as William Byrd, now began to compose music for the services of the Book of Common Prayer.

Summary

Where medieval worship had the Mass at its centre, the Reformers placed the sermon in that place of honour. Pews were placed in church buildings so that people could sit and listen to the sermons, lectures, and lessons, provided by the preachers who were understood primarily as "doctors of sacred scripture." The pulpit was placed in the centre of the church and in some cases it took the place of the Communion altar altogether. The Reformers transformed the church's worship space from "temple" to "auditorium" – a place to "hear the Word of the Lord." The Bible became the defining document for Protestants in all matters related to worship, though there was a variety in interpretation that contributed to diversity in worship practices. The sacraments were still very important to the Reformers and were not replaced by the Word. Luther and Calvin particularly retained a very high view of Baptism and the Lord's Supper as important means of grace. The liturgy was simplified but set forms of worship were still in place. The Church of England forged a synthesis of Catholic and Reformed emphases in its Book of Common Prayer. Musical styles in worship ranged from the unadorned singing of metrical versions of the Psalms to the rich and complex elaborate compositions of William Byrd.

Some Questions

1. Do you think Luther's "permissive" approach or Calvin's "restrictive" approach is best as a guide to worship? Why?

2. Worship styles impact on architectural arrangement. Is this evident in your own church setting? In what way does your worship space reflect your church's theology of worship?

3. What are the strengths and weaknesses of set prayers and liturgies on the one hand and an extemporary approach to worship on the other? Are there ways that both approaches can be brought together?

4. Assuming that legal sanctions against deviations from the norm in worship are a thing of the past, in what ways can churches exercise liturgical discipline? Is it proper to do so and if so how might it be carried out?

5. To what extent do your own church's worship practices reflect both Catholic and Reformed elements?

For Further Reading

Cummings, Brian, ed. *The Book of Common Prayer: The Texts of 1549, 1559 and 1662*. New York: Oxford University Press, 2012.

Davies, Horton. *Worship and Theology in England Volume1: From Cranmer to Hooker 1534-1603, Andrews to Baxter and Foxe, 1603-1690*. Cambridge: University Press, 1996.

MacCulloch, Diarmaid. *Thomas Cranmer: A Life*. New Haven, CT: Yale University Press, 1998.

Mitchell, Nathan D. "Reforms, Protestant and Catholic," ch. 8 in Geoffrey Wainwright,and Karen B. Westerfield-Tucker, eds. *The Oxford History of Christian Worship*. New York: Oxford University Press, 2005.

Sundberg, Walter. *Worship as Repentance: Lutheran Liturgical Tradition and Catholic Consensus*. Grand Rapids: Eerdmans, 2012.

Vischer, Lucas. *Christian Worship in Reformed Churches Past and Present*. Grand Rapids; Eerdmans, 2002.

Chapter Seven

Worship in the Age of Revivals: From Auditorium to Tent

A Uniting Church minister recounted the following on his congregation's website:

> Let me read to you a couple of letters that ministers have actually received when they tried to change hymn styles and bring in new music:
>
> 1. "What's wrong with the inspiring hymns with which we grew up: when I go to church, it is to worship God, not to be distracted with learning a new song. Last Sunday's was particularly unnerving. While the text was good, the tune was unsingable and the new harmonies were quite discordant."
>
> 2. "I am no music scholar, but I feel I know appropriate church music when I hear it. Last Sunday's new hymn, if you call it that, sounded like a sentimental love ballad one might expect to hear crooned in a saloon. If you persist in exposing us to rubbish like this in God's house, don't be surprised if many of the faithful look for a new place to worship. The hymns we grew up with are all we need."
>
> Those letters weren't actually written to ministers in our Presbytery. The first was written in 1890 and was complaining about "What a friend we have in Jesus." The second letter, dated 1865, was criticising the use of "Just as I am." The church we have always known, the way we have done things, worshipped and functioned, was itself responsible for changing the way previous generations had always done church. The Christian church has always been changing. We are fooling ourselves if we think we are the first generation to ever face change.[1]

While we cannot be certain which tunes were in use when these letters were written, the story reminds us that the "worship wars" are nothing new and that the church has always found innovation difficult to cope with. During the "modern period" (the period from Post-Reformation days, through the Enlightenment, and into the mid-twentieth century) the church underwent a bewildering rate of change in its worship patterns. We have a lot of ground to cover in surveying this period.

---

1   This was provided on the Belief Net website of the Brunswick (Victoria) Uniting Church but is no longer available at that source.

Pietist Hymnody

The German Pietist movement of the seventeenth century, sought to simplify religion, and tended to reject music as art. This brought them into conflict with the great German Lutheran composer Johann Sebastian Bach (1685-1750). Yet Bach was himself influenced by the Pietists. For example, his cantata texts reflect Pietist theology. One of the frequently recurring themes of Pietist hymnody is the relationship between Christ (the Groom) and the Church (his Bride). John Wesley would later take exception to some of the highly intimate language in these hymns, with their almost "erotic" overtones. (He did however translate many Pietist hymns for Methodist use.) English translations were often sanitised versions of the German originals. Modern German translations have also made significant changes. For example, Franck's *Jesu, meine Freude*, ("Jesus My Joy") modelled on H. Alberti's love song, "Flora my joy" originally read "Jesus, my *Zucker* (Sugar)." Charles Wesley's *Jesus, Lover of My Soul*, reflects this Pietist influence. His brother, John said that this hymn was so personal that it should not be sung in public worship. In spite of this, it has become one of the most widely sung of Charles' hymns.

The Hymns of Isaac Watts

As noted earlier, metrical versions of the Psalms were the preferred form in English church music after the Reformation. However, from the end of the seventeenth century, hymns began to appear in appendixes to Psalters, intended for private and home use. The Baptist minister Benjamin Keach was the first to introduce a hymn of "human composure" for use in a service of Holy Communion, in 1690. But the transition in English church music from psalm singing to hymn singing was really pioneered by the work of Isaac Watts (1674-1748). The story is told that as a young person he criticised the language of the metrical Psalms and when his father encouraged him to write his own if he though he could do better. he did so and went on to write over six hundred hymn texts.

Watts first began to write "free, Christianized psalms."[2] These were an attempt to give the Old Testament Psalms a Christological orientation and make them relevant to the Gospel age. His next move, the writing of original hymn texts, earned him the title of the "father of English hymnody." English hymns were sung in Presbyterian, Congregational, and Baptist churches for a full one hundred years before they found their way into Anglican usage. "Watts has been said to combine most successfully the expression of objective worship

---

2   Hustad, 206.

with that of subjective devotional experience...best illustrated in his well-known hymn, *When I Survey the Wondrous Cross.*"[3]

Methodist Worship

Methodist worship began as a kind of modified Anglicanism. "I believe there is no worship in the world," wrote John Wesley, "either in ancient or modern language, which breathes more of a solid, Scriptural, rational piety than the Common Prayer of the Church of England, and though the main of it was compiled more than 200 years ago, yet is the language of it not only pure but strong and elegant in the highest degree."[4]

Wesley expected Methodists in England fully to participate in the services of the Church of England, and forbade Methodists from holding their meetings during "church hours," in order to enable this participation. Such involvement was then to be supplemented by meetings in small groups (classes and bands) and by the preaching services of the Methodists. The Puritan concept of family worship was retained among the Methodists. Preachers were to fast Wednesdays and Fridays until 4pm, and quarterly fast days were to be held among the Methodists. The practice of Wednesday and Friday fasts was in imitation of the early church period when fasting vigils were held on Wednesdays to commemorate the day upon which Judas struck a deal with the Sanhedrin to betray Jesus, and Fridays in memory of the crucifixion.

The Love Feast was a rather unique means of spiritual nurture within early Methodism serving in the earliest period as a kind of substitute for the Eucharist. Prayer, hymn singing, exhortation and testimonies were accompanied by a simple, symbolic meal of bread and water shared between members as a sign of reconciliation. Special two-handled cups were manufactured, surviving examples of which provide an interesting example of the material culture of early Methodism. Wesley may have originally used bread and wine but, seeing the confusion that might be caused, substituted cake and water or tea.

Well into the nineteenth century the Love Feast continued to provide a context for a sense of divine visitation. In January 1835 William Schofield rode from his Windsor circuit to Sydney to attend a Love Feast presided over by Joseph Orton. Schofield 'made a few remarks upon the importance of waiting upon the Lord in holy expectation of receiving the accomplishment of his promises' and testified to a strong sense that the meeting should not end at the usual time while the power of the Lord was so strong upon the meeting. Orton agreed and the meeting continued till midnight before which time, in Schofield's words,

---

3   Hustad, 206.
4   John Wesley, *Works* (Jackson edition) 14:317.

'Brother Simpson and I were wholly sanctified.'[5] This incident illustrates the free-flowing supernaturalised nature of Methodist gatherings during this period, before being replaced by more formal structured services.

John Wesley borrowed the Covenant Service from Puritan practice, condensing the seventeenth century service composed by Richard Alleine. In an Arminian theological context where the security of one's salvation is dependent in part upon response to God's grace, an annual opportunity to renew one's covenant with God was a helpful device. The Covenant Service was typically held on the first Sunday of the year and it was often preceded by a New Years Eve "Watchnight" service.[6]

When the Methodist Episcopal Church was formed in America in 1784, Wesley abridged the Anglican Book of Common Prayer into *The Sunday Service of the Methodists in North America*. Most of the holy days ("so-called") were omitted. Frequent communion (weekly) was urged, and communion was seen as a "converting" as well as a "confirming" ordinance. Wesley's approach to the Table differed from the Puritan approach, in that he did not require that a person receiving Communion had experienced the new birth. "True penitents" could come to the Table, seeking prevenient, justifying, or sanctifying grace. Children as young as nine were to be admitted, and the usual practice was to receive from a kneeling position in groups gathered at the altar rail.

"Mr. Wesley's Abridgment" of the Book of Common Prayer was a greatly shortened form, and included altered services for special occasions. Godparents were omitted from the Office of Baptism, and the word "priest" was replaced with "minister." The word "regenerate" was omitted from the phrase, "this child is regenerate and grafted into the Body of Christ's Church." The sign of the cross over the baptised was omitted by Wesley, but added at a later date. There was no mention of the Rite of Confirmation, which was not widely used, even in the Anglicanism of Wesley's day. There is no mention of a ring in the "Solemnization of Matrimony." This may show a Puritan influence, with its rejection of the "wearing of gold and precious stones." A service of "Communion for the Sick" is included, as are services for the Burial of the Dead (interestingly, Wesley rejected

---

5   Schofield to Secretaries, 1 May 1835, cited in J. D. Bollen, "A Time of Small Things: The Methodist Mission in New South Wales, 1815-1836," *Journal of Religious History* 7:3 (June 1973), 231; Alex Tyrrell, *A Sphere of Benevolence: The Life of Joseph Orton, Wesleyan Methodist Missionary (1795-1842)* (Melbourne: State Library of Victoria, 1993), 87.

6   See William Parkes, "Watchnight, Covenant Service, and the Love Feast in Early British Methodism," in *Wesleyan Theological Journal*, vol. 32, no. 2 (Fall 1997), 35-58; and Lester Ruth, "A Little Heaven Below: The Love Feast and Lord's Supper in Early American Methodism, in *Wesleyan Theological Journal*, vol. 32, no. 2 (Fall 1997), 59-79.

the idea of "consecrated ground" for burial), and for Ordination. "Select Psalms" were included, and many of the "imprecatory" Psalms (those which called God's wrath down on the heads of enemies) were rejected as being not fit for the lips of a Christian congregation. The Thirty-Nine Articles of the Church of England were reduced to Twenty-Four.[7]

Wesley's Abridgement was not well received among American Methodists. One of the early Methodist preachers is known to have said, "Our preachers prefer to pray with their eyes shut," expressing a decided preference for extemporary over written prayers. Subsequently, Methodism in America developed in a more revivalist fashion, which included less sacramental observance, more extemporary prayer, and a focus on preaching, often to the neglect of other aspects of worship. The pattern was similar in Australian Methodism.

> The only written material a preacher took into the pulpit was his thumb-marked Bible and his sermon notes or manuscript. His prayer, the 'long prayer' after the first hymn, was supposed to be 'free' or 'extempore.' Although he might have given some thought to its content beforehand, the words were expected to flow as the Spirit moved him. It is safe to say that, apart from set prayers in a baptismal or communion service, no Methodist preacher in the 1880s would have dared to read a prayer.[8]

There were however, Methodists who still used Wesley's Sunday Service and valued the more formal dignity of its earlier Anglican roots. A Methodist service held in Melbourne in 1836 reflects Anglican usages. "At 11 o'clock the people of the settlement were assembled for Divine service…The liturgy was read by Mr [Joseph] Orton, the responses were led by James Simpson, Esq. The tunes were raised by Dr Thompson, afterwards of Geelong."[9]

In the British Methodism of which Australian Methodists were a part, "Church" Methodists (more oriented toward Anglican worship) and "Chapel" Methodists (more oriented toward Dissenting worship) represented these two trajectories, and both patterns continue to be represented in all Methodist bodies today.

---

7   The American Methodists added a twenty-fifth Article, which was an oath of allegiance to the government of the United States of America, newly formed under George Washington. For an excellent treatment of the doctrinal heritage that lay behind these Articles and the subsequent revisions to them among Methodists see Thomas C. Oden, *Doctrinal Standards in the Wesleyan Tradition* (Grand Rapids: Francis Asbury Press, 1988).

8   Arnold D. Hunt, *This Side of Heaven: A History of Methodism in South Australia* (Adelaide: Lutheran Publishing House, 1985), 150.

9   W.L. Blamires and John B. Smith, *The Early Story of the Wesleyan Methodist Church in Victoria: A Jubilee Volume* (Melbourne: Wesleyan Book Depot, 1886), 14.

The Hymns of Charles Wesley (1707-1788)

The Methodist standards of doctrine were officially John Wesley's *Standard Sermons* and *Explanatory Notes upon the New Testament*. To these must be added, even if *de facto*, the hymns of Charles Wesley. The 1780 collection of *Hymns for the Use of the People Called Methodists* has been ranked along with the *Book of Common Prayer* and the *Canon* of the Mass as one of the greatest liturgical resources ever written. John Wesley gives the following description in the book's Preface.

> It is large enough to contain all the important truths of our most holy religion, whether speculative or practical; yea, to illustrate them all and to prove them both by Scripture and reason; and this is done in a regular order. These hymns are not carelessly jumbled together, but carefully ranged under proper heads, according to the experience of real Christians. So that this book is, in effect, a little body of experimental and practical divinity...In what other publication of the kind do you have so distinct and full an account of Scriptural Christianity? Such a declaration of the heights and depths of religion, speculative and practical? So strong cautions against the most plausible errors?...and so clear directions for making your calling and election sure; for perfecting holiness in the fear of God?[10]

John Lawson has made a distinction between the "Scripture Hymns" of Wesley and Watts, and the later "Christian sentiment" hymns of the 19th Century.[11] J. Ernest Rattenbury reminds us that in Wesley's hymns we see theology as art and devotion.

> Religious doctrine is perhaps better approached and understood as art than as science; as penitent devotion than as desiccated dogma. If theology is discourse about God, it may be claimed that adoration is as important for its construction as reason. Charles Wesley was an adoring penitent, penitent as he adored, adoring as he was thankful...His method of expressing his discoveries about God was no less valuable because it was the artist's method and not the philosopher's or scientist's.[12]

---

10   John Wesley, Preface to *Hymns for the Use of the People Called Methodists* (1780). A critical edition of this hymn book edited by Franz Hildebrandt and Oliver A. Beckerlegge constitutes vol. 7 in the Bicentennial Edition of the Works of John Wesley (Nashville: Abingdon, 1983).

11   John Lawson, *A Thousand Tongues: The Wesley Hymns as a Guide to Scriptural Teaching* (Exeter: Paternoster, 1987), 11-20.

12   J. Ernest Rattenbury, *The Evangelical Doctrines of Charles Wesley's Hymns* (London: Epworth, 1941), 87. Reprinted by Burlington, IN: Meetinghouse Press, 2006.

Altogether Charles wrote some 6,500 hymns. His brother John edited these and was also responsible for the translation of a number of German pietist hymns, such as *Jesus, Thy Blood and Righteousness*. Poetically, the Wesleys helped liberate church music from the confines of the two-line metres – common, long, and short – that had become established patterns in both Anglican psalmody and Watts' hymnody. It has often been stated that the Wesley brothers took popular pub tunes of the day for the musical settings of their hymns. This is actually something of an urban myth. There is nothing in the literature to clearly demonstrate this. The error seems to have come about by mistaking the term "bar form" as a reference to pubs. Methodist scholar, Dean McIntyre has pointed out that the term is a musical reference to an AAB pattern in music, where the first two lines of a tune are identical and the third line varies. We do have one instance recorded where Charles overheard a group of drunken sailors singing a popular British folk song, which was distracting the crowd as he was trying to preach.

> Charles interrupted his sermon, pointed to the sailors out on the edge of the crowd and addressed them specifically, and invited them to return to the evening service and he would have a song that they really should sing. So that broke up the event, and the sailors went their way, and Charles went back to his apartment, that afternoon, and he penned the words of a hymn, the first line of which is "Listed into the cause of sin, why should a good be evil?" He wrote these words to the tune of *Nancy Dawson*. The other lyrics to the song say, 'Music alas too long has been, pressed to obey the devil. Drunken or lewd or light the lay, fell to the soul's undoing. Widen the truth with flowers alay, down to eternal ruin.' Today, the tune is also a popular nursery rhyme, entitled *Here We Go 'Round the Mulberry Bush*.[13]

So what *were* the early musical sources for most of the Wesley hymns? According to musicologist Donald Hustad, they were "the newer psalm tunes, opera melodies, and secular folk songs of German origin."[14] It is interesting to note how Wesley's hymns are found today in hymn books of all denominations – Roman Catholic, Anglican, Presbyterian, Baptist – a testament to their universal value and appeal. Wesleyan hymnody remain a rich mine of solid theological verse.

---

13   Dean B. McIntyre, "Did the Wesleys Really Use Drinking Tune Songs for their Hymns?" http://www.gbod.org/worship/default.asp?act=reader&item_id=2639/
14   Hustad, 208.

American Revivalism and Gospel Songs

Early colonists in North America included Spanish Catholics, who settled areas such as Saint Augustine, Florida (the oldest city in the US), the Caribbean islands, and Mexico. Music schools and cathedral choirs were established and American composers wrote masses in the style of Palestrina, Victoria, and di Lasso. A handful of Huguenots (French Protestants) in the colony of Georgia, brought the metrical Psalms of Calvin with them. French psalm tunes were taught to the Native Americans of the area. Further north, the Eastern seaboard colonists were primarily of British extraction. They brought with them the Sternhold and Hopkins Psalter, and the Ainsworth Psalter, produced in 1612 by English Protestants in exile in Amsterdam.

The *Bay Psalm Book* (1640), a revision of Psalm texts, was the first major publishing enterprise of the colonies. These were "lined out" by a deacon or precentor for the benefit of congregations who were illiterate or who had no books of their own. A very limited range of tunes was available, as the tunes tended to be passed on by oral tradition rather than be written down. In the early eighteenth century organs and choirs began to appear in rear balconies of larger churches. A cello or woodwind instrument might also be employed to assist the singing. Some churches established "singing schools" often led by talented musical amateurs. By the late eighteenth century "tune books" began to be published, containing British folk tunes. Some early American songwriters, such as William Billings (1746-1800), began to write original tunes.

The hymns of Wesley and Watts were sung by the Presbyterians and Congregationalists of New England. Watts' *The Psalms of David Imitated in the Language of the New Testament* (1729) was published by Benjamin Franklin. John Wesley, while a missionary in Georgia, published a *Collection of Psalms and Hymns* (1737) in Charleston, South Carolina, said to be the first hymnbook published in America. The evangelist George Whitefield's use of hymns, especially those of Isaac Watts, in his well attended open-air meetings helped to break down resistance to hymns.

Baptist churches in the Southern colonies developed two worship traditions, the more formal represented by The First Baptist Church of Charleston, South Carolina, and the more revivalistic by the Sandy Creek, (North Carolina) congregation. The Charleston congregation was the first Baptist church founded in the south (c.1695). In the eighteenth century it had retained a formal, stately (though evangelical) style of worship. Its members were known as "Regular" (i.e. "Calvinistic") Baptists. They sang the Psalms, Isaac Watts, and Baptist hymns written in a similar mould.

The Sandy Creek, North Carolina group were "Separate" (i.e. "Arminian") Baptists, led by the charismatic Shubal Stearns. Much more revivalistic in style, "ardor, not order" characterized their approach.[15] Instead of the Psalms and Watts' hymns they sang the lively folk hymns of the American frontier.

> Faith was feeling and every Sunday was a camp meeting. The praise of God was not vertical but horizontal. Unlike the city slickers at Charleston, they did not praise God by praising God; they praised God by reaching women and men. They had a mourner's bench and they expected public groaning not polite amens.[16]

Revivalist worship in the nineteenth century followed this more informal evangelistic model, whereby the church became a "tent," rather than a "temple." The pattern used by the YMCA in the 1850s came into wide use in the churches. A song service was followed by a brief prayer, announcements, choir or solo musical item, offering, solo, then sermon (the central focus of the service), followed by an invitation (often lengthy and accompanied by hymns) and dismissal. Charles Finney provided rules for what he considered a good revivalist liturgy. Increasingly older hymns of the Wesley and Watts era were replaced by the newer "gospel songs." Psalms were all too often completely ignored.

American music collections such as *Kentucky Harmony* (1816), *Southern Harmony* (1835) and *The Sacred Harp* (1844) contained songs that are now often referred to as "Early American folk melodies, "white spirituals," "Appalachian folk tunes," or "old Baptist music."[17] These are further examples of the sacred-secular borrowing already noted in earlier periods. A more urban phase of revivals was initiated under the ministry of Charles Finney in the first half of the nineteenth century (principally in the period 1824-1850). At this time the foundations of the Moody/Sankey and Graham/Shea combining of a preacher with a musician was established. Thomas Hastings (1784-1872) was a leading music teacher and conductor who, in association with Finney, compiled the first hymnbooks to be used specifically for use in his revivals.

The rise and growth of Sunday Schools led to the composition of children's songs in the camp meeting style, "with catchy, easily remembered melody, simple harmony and rhythm and an inevitable refrain."[18] The "Gospel Song" soon followed, first launched by the YMCA in the 1860s. Authors such as P. P. Bliss wrote in a similar style to the famous American songwriter Stephen

---

15   Hustad, 220.
16   Walter B. Shurden, "The Southern Baptist Synthesis: Is it Cracking?" in *Baptist History and Heritage* (April, 1981), 2-10.
17   Hustad, 225.
18   Hustad, 232.

Foster. Fanny Crosby had been a successful secular songwriter before she took pen to paper to compose her well-known Gospel songs, such as *Blessed Assurance*. The Gospel Song was defined in the early twentieth century as:

> A sacred folk song, free in form, emotional in character, devout in attitude, evangelistic in purpose and spirit. [They] are more or less subjective in their matter and develop a single thought, rather than a line of thought. That thought usually finds its supreme expression in the chorus or refrain which binds the stanzas together in a very close unity, just as it does in lyrical poetry where it is occasionally used.[19]

Though Gospel songs have folk music origins, Gospel songwriters were by no means unlettered rustics but were often sophisticated urbane professionals. Phoebe Palmer Knapp, who wrote the music for *Blessed Assurance*, was married to the President of the Metropolitan Life Insurance Company. Fanny Crosby's associate Howard Doane was a wealthy industrialist and civic leader. Robert Lowry was professor of literature at Bucknell University. Charles Converse, who wrote the music for *What a Friend We Have in Jesus*, studied in Europe where he met the composers Schumann and Liszt. Fanny Crosby was a close associate of five American presidents as well as other important civic leaders. The music these people composed often made them a great deal of money. This American development was soon exported overseas and gave rise to similar efforts in other countries such as among Swedish Lutherans.

Dwight L. Moody (1837-1899) and Ira D. Sankey (1840-1908) were the first "team-act" of evangelist and song leader. Their hugely successful campaign in Great Britain brought them on to the world stage. Moody understood the power of music as an agent of persuasion and he used it to good effect.[20] A magazine of the period *The Nation*, described the music of the Moody and Sankey crusades as follows: "Determine the pleasure that you get from a circus quick-step, a Negro-minstrel sentimental ballad, a college chorus, and a hymn all in one, and you have some gauge of the variety and contrast that may be perceived in one of these songs."[21] The invention of the harmonium rendered music leadership more democratic, and in both England and America signalled the beginning of the end for the use of bands in the upstairs balcony, which now began to be seen as obsolete.

---

19   Edmund Simon Lorenz, *Church Music: What a Minister Should Know About It* (New York: Fleming H. Revell, 1923), 342.

20   Bernard R. DeRemer. *Moody Bible Institute: A Pictorial History* (Chicago: Moody Press, 1960), 30.

21   *The Nation* 22 (9 March, 1876), 157 quoted in James F. Findlay Jr., *Dwight L. Moody: American Evangelist, 1837-1899* (Chicago: University of Chicago Press, 1969), 211.

It has sometimes been argued that hymns are more objective and God-centred and gospel songs more subjective and "human-centred." Yet many gospel songs are very objective and God-centred and many hymns are very subjective and focused on Christian experience (Charles Wesley's for example). The gospel song form had many strengths. These songs spoke of the saving love of God in Christ. They were couched in contemporary language. They were ballads, that is, narratives of human experience, which spoke to all who had shared a similar experience. They were emotionally infectious and their rhythmic patterns gave opportunity for such physical expressions as marching, clapping, and foot tapping, all enjoyable activities in the boisterous world of America's gilded age.

British Church Music of the Nineteenth Century

Where most of the hymn writers of the seventeenth and eighteenth centuries were concerned to present doctrine in their hymns, nineteenth century hymn writers, influenced by the spirit of the Romantic Age, were more interested in recording human religious experience. Not all of these were revivalists however. Many English church leaders of the nineteenth century attempted to write hymns in what they considered a more poetic and exalted literary style. Often this Romantic spirit, with its design for eliciting religious emotion had little interest in the direct text of scripture focusing more on the imagination and fancy of the human experience. Important hymn writers of this period include Reginald Heber, 1783-1826 (*Holy, Holy, Holy*); John Keble, 1792-1866 (*Sun of My Soul*); Henry Francis Lyte, 1793-1847 (*Abide With Me*); Sir John Bowring, 1792-1872 (*In the Cross of Christ I Glory*); Sir Robert Grant, 1779-1838 (O Worship the King); and Charlotte Elliot, 1789-1871 (*Just As I Am*).

On July 14, 1833 a new religious movement in England was launched when John Keble preached a sermon at Oxford entitled "National Apostasy." The Oxford (or "Tractarian") Movement was concerned that the English Church was being held captive by its connection to the Parliament of the day. It sought to affirm the catholicity and apostolicity of the Church of England as a church founded by Christ, and favoured the worship style of the pre-Reformation church. Its devotees were referred to as "High Church." Evangelicals ("Low Church" Anglicans) strongly rejected this movement as "popish." Some of its leaders, such as John Henry Newman, later converted to Roman Catholicism (Newman was made a cardinal), but most stayed in the Church of England. The Oxford Movement returned much of pre-Reformation worship styles to the Reformed churches of Britain – reviving the ancient Greek and Latin hymns, in English translations, and Gregorian chant. At the same time, like the revivalists, it had its populist side focused on the Mass. Both movements owed much to Romanticism with their stress on religious experience, the love of God and the aesthetics of the divine.

Its stress on dignified worship also influenced other Protestants in the Free Church tradition. Presbyterians, Methodists and Baptists all had their more "High Church" expressions, and each had a party that frowned upon such developments as leaning too far toward "Rome" and as not conducive to the preaching of the Gospel. Boys' choirs were established; liturgical vestments began to be worn by a greater number of Free Church clergy; ritual became more elaborate, with the use of anthems, processionals, and recessionals. Hymn writers produced by this movement include John Henry Newman, 1801-1890 (*Lead, Kindly Light*); Edward Caswell, 1814-1878 (*When Morning Gilds the Skies*); and John Mason Neale, 1818-1866 (*The Day of Resurrection*). William Faber, 1814-1863 (*Faith of Our Fathers, Living Still*); and Matthew Bridges, 1800-1863 (*Crown Him With Many Crowns*) joined Newman in leaving Anglicanism to join the Roman Catholic Church, becoming quite prominent leaders. *Hymns Ancient and Modern* (1861) was partly the product of Tractarianism and it would dominate Anglican hymn singing for over a hundred years.

Of course, these same patterns were replicated in the colonies. Nineteenth and early-twentieth century worship in Australia was a microcosm of the larger British world of which it was a part, and also received American influences from visiting evangelists who brought their "racy hymns" with them.[22] Presbyterians were sometimes wary of the sensual power of music to distract the worshipper from a focus on God, and often preferred unaccompanied singing of psalms.[23] Wesleyans were decidedly more enthusiastic in embracing hymns, choral music, and instrumental performances as a stimulus to worship.[24] Room was made for both "high brow" and "low brow" musical styles and in more informal settings such as prayer meetings, musicians even had room for improvisation.[25] One turn-of-the-century Methodist minister who embraced more "high-brow" music was Edward H. Sugden. The first Master of Queen's College in the University of Melbourne, Sugden patronised classical musical performances (unusual for a Methodist minister in his day and drawing some criticism from his colleagues), was a music critic

---

22   Richard Broome, *Treasure in Earthen Vessels: Protestant Christianity in New South Wales Society 1900-1914* (Brisbane: University of Queensland Press, 1980), 66.
23   Anne Doggett, "'The Old Vexed Question': Divergent Attitudes and Practices in the Sacred Music of Early Ballarat," *Journal of Religious History* 33:4 (Dec 2009), 417.
24   Doggett, 417.
25   Graeme Pender, "Improvisatory Music Practices in the Wesleyan Methodist Tradition," *Aldersgate Papers* 6 (Sept 2006), 8-33. This interesting article examines the musical practices among Wesleyan Methodists of Victoria from 1835-1914.

for the *Argus* and *Australasian* newspapers, and wrote hymn texts, tunes and arrangements for use in Methodist Sunday Schools and churches.[26] Catholic churches in colonial Victoria were the most embracing of the musical arts, utilising the sacred music of the great composers as central to the liturgy.[27] Anglicans were often divided over the use of music, especially those more ornate settings which could be seen as leaning too much toward Tractarianism. Bishop Charles Perry expressed his concern in the pages of the *Melbourne Church News* in 1867.

> While it is right to render the services of the Church cheerful, and, for this purpose to make due use of music, and lights, and decorations, care must be taken not to deceive ourselves by supposing that God is worshipped, while in reality only the lust of the eye, or the lust of the ear, in things pertaining to Divine Service is gratified.[28]

It is clear from these divergent approaches to worship in colonial Australia that not a lot has changed when it comes to disputes over what is or is not appropriate in the musical life of the church.

Summary

John and Charles Wesley had a great love for the liturgy of the Church of England which seemed to preserve the best elements of both pre-and post-Reformation worship. Later revivalists adopted a more populist (appealing to the "masses") approach. The basic service of the outdoor camp meeting (especially in America) began to replace the historic pattern of the liturgy (though it is important to remember that the American camp meeting has precedents in the outdoor sacramental services of Scottish Presbyterians and English Methodists.) Worship was now a matter of singing lively songs, preaching a sermon designed to get a decision, and giving an invitation to come forward to the altar. It was "the camp meeting come to town" and the older pattern of Entrance, Hearing, Responding, and Dismissal tended to be obscured. Nineteenth Century revivalists were quite deliberately minimalist in their liturgy, seeking a maximum impact in conversions. Songs were deliberately lightweight on doctrine and the venting of emotions was embraced as a helpful tool in conversion. A movement "from temple to auditorium" and "from auditorium to tent" had taken place among Evangelicals, and in all the denominational traditions diversity of worship was a feature that could sometimes lead to disruption.

---

26 D'Arcy Wood, "Composer, Arranger and Hymn Writer," Therese Radic, "Musician and Music Critic," chs. 12 and 13 in Renate Howe, ed. *The Master: The Life and Work of Edward H. Sugden* (Melbourne: Uniting Academic press, 2009), 157-66, 167-78.

27 Doggett, 413-15.

28 *Melbourne Church News*, 16 January 1867, cited in A. de Q. Robin, *Charles Perry, Bishop of Melbourne* (Nedlands, WA: University of Western Australia Press, 1967), 136-138.

Some Questions

1. John Wesley took exception to some of the highly intimate language of the German Pietist hymns, because they had almost "erotic" overtones. Can you think of any contemporary songs today that seem a little overly "romantic" or "intimate" in tone?

2. Does the worship of your church fit the First Baptist, Charleston, or Sandy Creek Baptist model? Or something else? Explain.

3. Classic hymns such as those of Isaac Watts are often put forward as good examples of "theology in song" having a certain depth to them often lacking in modern songs. However, there certainly are at least some good modern songs with solid theological content. What are some that you can bring to mind and in what way do they show good theology?

4. It has been said, "You can sing *Amazing Grace* to the tune of the Beach Boys' *California Girls* because the metre is the same (the lines have the same number of syllables). But why would you *want* to?" Respond to this statement.

For Further Reading

Chapman, David M. *Born in Song: Methodist Worship in Britain*. Warrington: Church in the Marketplace, 2006.

Chilcote, Paul W. "A Faith that Sings: The Renewing Power of Lyrical Theology," in Paul W. Chilcote, ed. *The Wesleyan Tradition: A Paradigm for Renewal*. (Nashville: Abingdon, 2002), 148-162.

Davies, Horton. *Worship and Theology in England Volume 2: From Watts and Wesley to Maurice 1690-1850, Newman to Matrineau 1850-1900* Cambridge: University Press, 1996.

Ellis, Christopher J. *Gathering: A Theology and Spirituality of Worship in Free Church Tradition*. London: SCM Press, 2004.

Westerfield Tucker, Karen. *American Methodist Worship*. Oxford: Oxford University Press, 2001.

CHAPTER EIGHT

Worship in the Modern and Post-modern World: From Tent to Kaleidoscope

Worship in the Twentieth Century

A great spirit of optimism was prevalent at the beginning of the twentieth century. It was thought that this would be the "Christian Century," and an important mainline periodical took that as its title. This optimism was shattered considerably by the experience of two world wars in the first half of a century that would prove to be just as warlike and marked by human greed and injustice as previous centuries. However the Christian Church continued to grow in the twentieth century especially in the southern hemisphere, with Asian, African, and Latin American Christianity exploding in growth and influence while the old line churches in Europe dwindled. The exception to this southern hemisphere dominance is the United States where Christianity has remained very strong, though even there it has felt the impact of secularism and atheism. Both Protestants and Catholics appropriated new technologies and used them enthusiastically. The invention of radio and television greatly affected worship as the church began increasingly to adjust its modes of communication to fit a new media-savvy culture. The organ began to be replaced by the piano (and later the keyboard). The more percussive sound of the piano seemed better suited to the lively gospel songs of the early twentieth century.

The American church music scene early in the century was dominated by the influence of D. B. Towner at Moody Bible Institute. Towner and his protégés took a biblical-theological approach to the content of their songs. This changed a little with the popularity of converted major league baseball player Billy Sunday, who along with his musical offsider and song leader-soloist-trombonist, Homer Rodeheaver brought a more "entertainment"-based style to evangelism. Sunday's physical antics and boisterous preaching was matched by Rodeheaver's invitation for railway workers to sing "I've been working on the railroad," and college crowds were invited to sing their school songs to new Christian words. All this was designed to put the crowds on side with the evangelists and their message, but it did mean that the earlier biblical-theological approach was diluted.

The memory of the Titanic was still in everyone's minds when the church sang songs such as "I was sinking deep in sin, far from the peaceful shore [but] love lifted me…" Testimony based songs were popular - "What a wonderful change in my life has been wrought since Jesus came into my heart…" A hymn from the 1920s reflected memories of trench warfare.

> Over the top for Jesus, bravely we will go,
> Over the top for Jesus, routing every foe;
> Never delaying when we hear the bugle blow,
> We'll fight for the right with all our might
> As over the top we go.

Radio "contributed to the passive character of recreation in our culture, and undoubtedly encouraged spectatorism in church life."[1] Merrill Dunlop (b. 1905) wrote gospel songs inspired by jazz rhythms and harmonies. He used the "rhumba" for hymns to be sung in a Latin American mission context. Moody Bible Institute began gospel broadcasting in 1926 using hymns written in a "sanctified broadway style."[2] After the Second World War, Youth for Christ rallies became popular in America. The chorus section of earlier gospel songs was often sung divorced from the stanzas, resulting in the musical form we now know as the "chorus." Youth For Christ employed the first ever approach to evangelism as marketed to a particular age niche. The most popular of these post-war Youth for Christ evangelists was a young Billy Graham, and his bass-baritone sidekick George Beverly Shea.

The Oxford Movement of the nineteenth century had something of a parallel in the twentieth century in the Liturgical Renewal Movement. Many leading liturgists and church music authorities began to call the church back to a more classical style of music in worship. They preferred Gregorian chant and "high art" musical forms to more "popular" approaches. But the use of popular music remained the dominant approach among Evangelicals. The Billy Graham Crusades have utilised the popular musical styles of each decade to complement the preaching of Dr. Graham. Bill and Gloria Gaither have been hugely popular as they have taken the latest secular pop and country songs and composed religious replies. Eugene L. Brand has said that the liturgical movement has been diverted from its "preoccupation with history (what is proper?) to a more pastoral concern (what is relevant?)."[3]

The Second Vatican Council revolutionised worship patterns in the Roman Catholic Church providing for greater participation of the people. The Latin Mass went into something of an eclipse and the vernacular was widely adopted. Altars were relocated so that the priest could stand behind a free standing

---

1 Donald P. Hustad, *Jubilate II: Church Music in Worship and Renewal* (Carol Stream: Hope Publishing, 1993), 251.

2 Hustad, 252.

3 Eugene L. Brand, *The Rite Thing* (Minneapolis: Augsburg, 1970), 56.

Table, facing toward rather than away from the people.[4] Transcendence had been replaced by immanence with an unprecedented stress on the Holy Spirit's activity among the people.

The following are some contributing influences on worship in the second half of the twentieth century:

1. Existentialist philosophy/theology with an emphasis on the "now" of experience.

2. The motto of the media commentator Marshall McLuhan was "the medium *is* the message." Advertising has less stress on words and rational argument and more on impressionistic visual images. An age of electronics, computers, television, and the internet has produced a more emotive/intuitive culture dependent on visual images more than rational argument.

3. "Secular" theology with its "religionless Christianity" has insisted that the church must divest itself of its own historic cultural forms and lose itself in service to the community.

4. Relational theology with its stress on fellowship and the priesthood of all believers has created a new sense of egalitarianism where clergy are no longer seen as those who are best equipped to bring their professional expertise to worship planning and implementation. "Why should the preacher do it all? Let's give Joe a go up on the platform."

5. Aesthetic relativism has led to a postmodern loss of "authority" in high art, and the triumph of "pop art" including kitsch (the idea that some art is so "bad" that it's "good"). There are no longer "experts" in art and culture. What I like is what is best. An *Amazing Spider-man* comic book is just as good as Shakespeare's *Macbeth* and The Beatles are as good as Bach.

6. The triumph of ecumenism and of Evangelicalism and Pentecostalism as trans-denominational movements, has led to a declining denominational loyalty and a loss of interest in both doctrinal distinctives and their accompanying liturgical traditions.

7. Consumerism means that no authority is recognized except that of personal choice. More or less instant gratification of personal needs is expected.

---

4   The rationale for the earlier position was that the priest faced the same direction as the people, that is, toward God whose presence was symbolised at the east of the sanctuary where the altar was situated.

Charismatic Worship

The Charismatic movement has introduced a fresh approach to the use of "contemporary music" in worship services. Pentecostals and Charismatics have argued that typical mainline Protestant worship has been too "cognitive-rational" in its emphasis. Charismatic worship has been identified, on the other hand, as more "intuitive-emotional."

The biblical basis for Charismatic worship practices is drawn primarily from the Old Testament, and in particular from David's Tabernacle, with its emphasis on singing, dancing, and instrumental music in the presence of the Ark of the Covenant, the symbol of God's living presence. Charismatic Christians typically define "worship" more narrowly than other believers. For most Christians, "worship" is all that takes place in the gathering of believers. For many Pentecostals and Charismatics, thanksgiving, praise, and worship are separate and consecutive movements. Preparation for worship begins in the "outer court" where *thanksgiving* is expressed. The gatherers then move to the "holy place" where *praise* is offered. Finally *worship* is reached where the focus is no longer on what God has done, but on adoring God for who God is. This often leads to a time of glossalalia (praising God in "tongues" or "singing in the Spirit"), and the utterance of "prophetic words." This pattern of concentrically smaller courts leading to a high point in the Holy of Holies is clearly based on the Old Testament tabernacle worship and some Pentecostal preachers see this renewal as a restoration of the "Davidic" pattern.

According to Hardy and Ford, praise and worship are often seen as a better approach to growth in sanctification than traditional Christian disciplines.[5] This desire to transcend discipline and the means of grace in a more direct, "unmediated" manner is a typical expression of Christian mysticism. This should give us pause, however. If God has chosen to mediate his grace to us through constituted means, is the transcendence of such means of grace a good thing?

You may have heard a distinction made between "praise and worship" and wondered what the difference is between the two things, if any. Pentecostals often want to make a distinction between thanking God for what God has done (praise) and worshipping God for who he is, quite separately from anything that he has done (worship). Paul Waitman Hoon gives a powerful theological critique of the concept that "pure" worship is attributing praise to God on the basis of his *worth* (who he is) quite separate from his *actions* (what he has done). "It is precisely the recital of, and engagement with, a particular

---

5   Daniel W. Hardy and Daniel F. Ford, *Praising and Knowing God* (Philadelphia: The Westminster Press, 1985), 82.

history bound up with a particular Jew, in a particular land, at a particular time that is the basis of Christian worship."[6] Indeed, Geoffrey Wainwright reminds us that creeds are also praise. "The motive or purpose of…confession is both doxology and witness. The act of confession is part of a more ample movement, a broader sweep which takes its origin in God and comes to completion in God, having drawn humanity to salvation during its course."[7]

Charismatic worship has an almost unvarying pattern of a lengthy period of contemporary praise and worship songs, followed by preaching, and then prayer ministry at the front of the church. Music plays a very large part in the entire liturgy. The earliest charismatic "choruses" were actually pioneered down under, in New Zealand, before impacting the church on a global scale. David and Dale Garratt released a 45rpm record in 1968 out of which emerged the popular *Scripture in Song* and *Songs of the Kingdom* series. Australasia has continued to be at the forefront of worship music, with the very widely used Hillsong material from the Hills Christian Church in Sydney.

The fresh approach to music that the Charismatic movement has introduced has much to commend it, especially in moving away from earlier "sentimentalised" gospel songs, overly subjective in nature, to the singing of biblical texts and songs of praise, often drawn from the psalms. On the other hand, the practice of repeating a simple chorus over and over in a kind of Christian "mantra" does have its problems. Many churches have dispensed with more theologically adequate "content" songs in favour of "praise" songs that are in themselves valid expressions of adoration, but do not teach much of anything at all. There is also a certain sameness about a generic pattern of worship that opens its franchises in every nave. It's a sad thing to visit churches of rich and various musical traditions and find that, instead of drawing from their own musical heritage, or from the latent compositional talent that exists in the congregation, they are all singing the same songs from the big worship music franchises. There is a kind of globalisation or monopoly taking place in which local product is not given the opportunity to emerge, a kind of "bland leading the bland." Much contemporary worship music is in the American "soft rock" style of FM radio, while a wide variety of "world music" styles are barely touched upon. This leads to a loss of musical diversity through the neglect of a wider range of musical styles.

---

6   Paul Waitman Hoon, *The Integrity of Worship* (Nashville: Abingdon Press, 1971), 91-94.

7   Geoffrey Wainwright, *Doxology: The Praise of God in Worship, Doctrine and Life* (New York: Oxford University Press, 1980), 182.

Evangelical churches have also largely opted for a full-blown appropriation of contemporary music forms. The "folk rock" phenomenon of the mid-sixties meant that everybody was keen to express his or her vision of the world, set to a simple musical accompaniment. Self-appointed prophets abounded and anyone with a guitar could be a "singer songwriter" with his or her own unique take on the meaning of things. By the 1980s Christian contemporary music was outselling its secular counterpart in the United States, meaning that a Christian artist could have phenomenal success without every breaking out of a Christian constituency. To country, pop, and rock forms of Gospel music have been added rap, ska, r & b, metal, grunge, "alternative" etc. There is even Christian punk and Christian "death metal" (!)

In popular music, simpler musical forms are preferred to more complex ones. There is a corresponding decline in musical education at all levels. Some Christian commentators have seen rock music as a product of a culture of protest and rebellion, a culture determined by reaction and demand, rather than by trans-generational mentoring, and the passing on of time-honoured cultural forms.[8] This is not the whole story, and the positive role of rock music in helping generations of people find a "voice" of legitimate protest and the championing of social justice and freedom should also be kept in mind. Nonetheless, there is a "dark side" to every musical form of which we should remain aware.

It is important to protect musical education in the life of the church. More and more in the public school system music is no longer taught and parents who want their children to learn music must pay for extra-curricular lessons. The preference for words-only OHP and Power Point presentations, rather than the hymnbook, means that people are no longer reading any kind of musical text. Whereas in previous times people learned to read music in church, this is less and less the case. Any local church with a musically gifted person and the ability and time to teach music has a valuable asset. The formation of a choir is one way to enhance musical appreciation and ability in the local church. Worship band rehearsals are so much more fruitful if there is a bandleader with training in music who can guide the musicians to improve their musical literacy and skills.

Some positives about charismatic worship:

- The insistence that worshipping God should take a very high priority in a believer's life is certainly commendable.
- Worship should be the work of all the people, not just the clergy, and

---

8   Hustad, 280–81.

charismatic worship gives plenty of opportunity for congregational involvement through the practice of spiritual gifts (though it is still pretty much led by those on the "platform").

- Worship should involve the whole person including the body and the emotions and there is a physical and emotional abandon in charismatic worship that provides a channel for such expression. If kept within the biblical command of worshipping in an "orderly" fashion, this can be a very positive thing.

Some reservations about charismatic worship:

- The idea that God is somehow more fully God as a result of our praise is to be rejected. There is a popular chorus with the line, "and in our worship build your throne." This is bad, or at least sloppy, theology as the throne of God (a symbol of God's rule) is not dependant in any way upon our worship.
- The New Testament, rather than the Old, should be the defining source for Christian worship. Christ and his finished work is the centre of our worship, not David's Tabernacle or Solomon's Temple.
- Though stressing transcendence, charismatic worship often lacks a true sense of mystery, penitence, humility, and awe, and can sometimes have the appearance of manipulating God and the crowd through "techniques."
- There is often too little stress on the theological content of the faith in charismatic worship.
- The idea that charismatic renewal music is a fulfilment of such texts as Joel 2:28 and Acts 2:17 is based on very poor interpretation of the Bible.
- The often-heard idea that charismatic renewal songs are "new wine" and classic hymns are "old wine" (apart from being a very poor application of a verse taken out of context) leads to a significant cultural loss of the church's tradition. "When we sing the hymns of Ambrose and Luther and Wesley, we give witness to the perpetuity of God's covenant as well as the continuity of the Spirit's presence."[9]
- Worship is impoverished when its music lacks excellent melodic and harmonic elements, theologically valid texts, and musical artistry.
- The "demographic" approach with a focus almost exclusively on the needs of the young, lacks the breadth that a more biblical, theological and historic study of worship would bring.

---

9   Hustad, 296.

How are we to respond to all this?

- Rather than being uncritically influenced by the "McWorship" franchise of contemporary music, we need to take the responsibility to study worship, becoming theologically literate about our liturgical practice and etiquette. Reading this book is one way of doing that.

- We should ensure that the Scriptures are given a major role in our worship and that we include Old and New Testament readings from a variety of biblical genres – psalms, history, epistles, Gospels, apocalyptic. The preaching, prayer, acts of dedication, and musical expressions should all be related to these readings in a full service of Word and Table wherever possible.

- The language used in our worship should be scriptural. We need not shy away from using distinctively Christian language in our worship, as this is the language that best conveys our story. Jesus is not our "life coach" or our "boss" – he is Lord and Saviour and our worship should reflect this Christian distinctiveness.

- Conform to the basics of the four-fold pattern in the historic liturgy.

  1. A pattern of entrance involving a distinctively Christian greeting and call to worship.
  2. A hearing of God's Word, read and expounded.
  3. A response to God's Word.
  4. A dismissal involving a benediction and commissioning into the world for mission.

- Do not follow the crowd or the latest fads; follow God. A young pastor told me (in 1999) that they do not sing any songs more than five years old, because they wanted to be "a church of the nineties." Given that he had one year to go before the nineties was over, I wondered what kind of church they would want to be after that! It has been said that the church that marries its own generation becomes a widow in the next.

- Express joy; let visitors sense the power of Christ among God's people. Part of the appeal of charismatic worship is the expression of joy that is often present. This often has a great evangelistic impact as people are drawn to a positive atmosphere. As Sally Morgenthaler has said, "Unbelievers come to church, not primarily to investigate the claims of Christ, but to investigate the Christ in us."[10]

- Guard important symbols, such as the cross, and do not replace them

---

10   Sally Morgenthaler, "Worship Evangelism: Bring Down the Walls," in *Worship Leader*, I:6.

with secular ones. Some churches have removed all religious symbols from their sanctuaries, not wanting to offend or confuse any visitors. Yet the fact remains that the cross is one of the most universally recognised symbols of the Christian faith. We need not be embarrassed or apologetic about it. Many non-churched people, even in a world no longer dominated by a Christian worldview, find great meaning and significance in traditional religious symbols and expect to find them in Christian places of worship.

- Changes to worship should unite, not divide, congregations. Liturgical change is often necessary but it is fraught with difficulty. Sometimes people with an agenda to introduce Charismatic renewal to an unwilling congregation can cause a church to fracture and split into competing parties. On the other hand ultra-traditionalists can stubbornly refuse even the most innocent of suggested changes more out of fear than out of careful thought.

- Include "teaching moments" about worship in the service itself. This is a special responsibility of congregational leaders, but song leaders and others who lead worship can also inject brief moments of explanation on the theological significance of the actions we take. There should not be a running commentary on everything that is happening but rather an occasional moment of pausing to explain, for example, why we stand when the Gospel is read, or why we take up the offering after, instead of before, the sermon. Socrates said that "the unexamined life is not worth living." It might also be said that "unexamined worship is not worth giving." Paul spoke in Romans 12:1-2 about offering our "spiritual service of worship." The phrase is a single word in the Greek and includes the root word "logos" which means "word" or "reason." One translation renders it "your rational worship." There are reasons why we do what we do and we ought to be able to explain those reasons. Otherwise we just become part of a mindless crowd mimicking actions without true understanding.

Alt.Worship

Alt.worship (Alternative worship) is characterised by a kaleidoscope of images and styles and seeks to take seriously the cultural trends that generally go under the umbrella term of "Postmodernism." Now here is where many readers may groan because I have used that groan-worthy word "postmodernism." As much of a cliché as that word is, and as much as it is a word that often gets thrown around without much definite meaning, it *is* something we have to take into consideration in our study of worship where postmodern modes of communication are now often taken for granted. It is difficult to continue the metaphor of different types of architecture that we have followed up to this point. Perhaps the closest we could come would be a fun house or house of mirrors where a multiplicity of images dazzle the senses from all directions. It is important to distinguish between Postmodernism *as a philosophy* and postmodernity *as a cultural trend*. Most of what is said by popular Christian writers about Postmodernism and its impact on the church relates more to the cultural trend than to the philosophy. When viewed as a cultural shift Postmodernism seems to me to be indistinguishable from the movement known as "Romanticism." The preference for nature over the machine, for poetry over facts, for imagination over knowledge and for emotions over thoughts is deeply embedded in western culture. Such preferences do not begin to make their presence felt only in the last fifty years. If one were to attempt to trace this development historically one would do better to begin in the 1860s than the 1960s. So the shifting of our cultural landscape in such ways is not something altogether new, but has been with us for a long time. Though it is often overstated and made simplistic it remains true that such a cultural shift has taken place. This is not bad news for the church because much of what Postmodernism says, the church has always said in any case, and the Gospel is as relevant to the post-modern person as it was to the modern person or to the person of the ancient world. To understand the term 'postmodern' we must first define what is meant by 'modern.'

The Modern Outlook[11]

Modernism was characterised by a number of features:

- Individualism and the assertion of personal autonomy.
- Rationalism with its confidence in the mind adequately to interpret reality without reference to external authorities such as church and tradition.
- Factualism which asserts the possibility of the individual using reason to arrive at objectively verifiable truths of all kinds.

These were the foundational views of a cultural movement in Europe beginning in the eighteenth century known as "the Enlightenment." This movement produced three convictions, shared by modern Christians and non-Christians alike:

- Foundationalism – "the philosophical and theological conviction that there are beliefs or experiences that are in themselves beyond doubt

---

11   Much of this material is drawn from Robert E. Webber, *Ancient-Future Faith: Rethinking Evangelicalism for a Postmodern World* (Grand Rapids: Baker, 1999).

and upon which systems of belief and understanding can therefore be constructed with certainty."[12]

- Structuralism – "the belief that societies construct texts to make meaning out of life and that the meaning which is in the text can be commonly agreed upon by its interpreters through the use of reason."[13]
- The Notion of the Metanarrative – the stories of the text that help make sense out of life and of the world.

Both liberal and conservative Christians have shared all of these assumptions to a large extent. The revelation of God in Jesus Christ is their foundationalism. They believe that the existence of God can be given rational proofs and that the resurrection of Christ and the historical accuracy of the Bible should be subject to the scientific and historical method. The Bible contains their "meta-narrative" which helps makes sense of the world and it should be interpreted using the historical and grammatical method. Many Christians are modernists in all of these respects. However, along with modernist assumptions, the church has also always known things which post-modernists may think of as new but which are not really new at all, having roots in very ancient ways of thinking.

The Post-Modern Outlook

In recent times, there has been a shift in scientific discourse toward the idea of *interpreted* fact. The old certainties of Newtonian physics – such as that the universe runs according to more or less fixed laws – are crumbling. The new scientific theory of "chaos" with its view that the so called laws of physics reflect only what is *most often* observed rather than what *must always* occur, is an example of this shift. Evolutionists remain convinced that human evolution took place but they are far less confident than they once were about *how* it did so, and many aspects of the older Darwinism have been superseded by fresh theories.

Alongside these changes in scientific outlook has been an equally significant philosophical shift toward affirming "the dialogical interaction of all things."[14] The notion of absolutes has been challenged. The universe is seen as a web of relationships, no single one of which holds the key to meaning. One result of this outlook has been pluralism which must make room for a multiplicity

---

12   John E. Thiel, *Nonfoundationalism* (Minneapolis: Fortress, 1994), cited in Paul Lakeland, *Postmodernity: Christian Identity in a Postmodern Age* (Minneapolis: Fortress, 1997), 125.

13   Webber, *Ancient-Future Faith*, 19. See also Claude Levi-Strauss, *Structural Anthropology* (New York: Basic Books, 1958).

14   Webber, *Ancient-Future Faith*, 22. See Mikhail M. Bakhtin, *The Dialogic Imagination*, ed. Michael Holquist, trans. Caryl Emerson and Michael Holquist (Austin: University of Texas Press, 1981).

of viewpoints even if they should appear mutually exclusive. The authority of language has been attacked (especially by Jacques Derrida, and his "deconstruction" of texts).[15] Truths may be true for one person and not true for another, or may only be true if they are "useful for the moment" (Richard Rorty). The "metanarratives" of particular communities cannot be applied outside of that community.[16]

At first this may not sound like a very Christian way of viewing the world but if we think about it a little further we find that it actually shares a great deal with the Christian outlook. The Christian story affirms that there is indeed an inter-relatedness to all things, that creation is a complex network of connections put in place and sustained by God. The distance between the spiritual and material worlds is not that great, as there are principalities and powers that inhabit the invisible world and have their impact for good and for evil on this visible world in which we live. Christians certainly need not give up the idea of absolute truth but they do strongly affirm that no one person or church organization can possess that absolute truth absolutely. It was a major conviction of the Protestant Reformers that the Medieval Catholic Church's claim to be the possessor, through its teaching office, of absolute truth, was indefensible. To the idea that there was no other way to understand the Gospel than that understanding enshrined in the Church's canon law, the Reformers rightly said "no." Christian theology agrees with postmodernism that institutions are not be completely trusted and we are taught in the Gospel to be aware of those language games that people in power will play to shore up their power in order to exert it over others.

The post-modern idea that language constructs reality and that we are all shaped by the telling of particular stories is also at the heart of what it means to be the people of God. Christians are a people called into being by God gathered around a particular story – the Exodus narrative – having been delivered from the kingdom of darkness and transferred to the kingdom of light through the cross and the empty tomb. Christians do not worship some vague Divine Principle but a particular God – a God with a Name and with a history. Christians also agree with the postmodern claim that the grand stories of particular communities cannot be applied universally to all. That is not to say that the Gospel isn't true for all people, but to recognise that a person must be converted, a person must be formed and transformed by the Spirit of

---

15   Jacques Derrida, *Of Grammatology* (Baltimore: Johns Hopkins University Press, 1997).
16   In light of all this Hans-Georg Gadamer has called for a rehabilitation of the concepts of Tradition, Authority, and Prejudice. Hans-Georg Gadamer, *Truth and Method* (New York: Continuum, 1998).

God in the community of God's people before he or she can ever understand what the Gospel is all about. If we are willing to admit it, we are all group product. Each of us is who we are because of the network of relationships that has nurtured us and shaped us into who we are today. We are all members of a particular community – not just the *human* community, where we might find more or less universally applicable truths, but the *Christian* community – where we are shaped by *particular* truths. In addition some of us belong to a particular community known as "Presbyterian" which has a somewhat different story to the particular community called "Baptist," and then to our particular local churches as well, with their own unique stories. All of this is very postmodern but at the same time as ancient as Genesis chapter 12 when God first called Abraham and decided to make from him a family that would bless all the nations of the earth, extending God's blessing from the particular to the universal.

In the area of communications, we now inhabit a much more *visual* culture than the modern period proved to be. Since the invention of the printing press the written word had been king, but the invention of cinema and later television, though modern technology, has taken us back, ironically, to a more ancient visual culture with a focus on pictures, on narrative and on storytelling. On 7 January 1839, members of the French Academy of Sciences were shown the first rudimentary photographs thus changing the visual arts forever. This remarkable invention was the work of the Parisian painter and printmaker Louis-Jacques-Mandé Daguerre who manipulated light to capture unique images on highly polished, silver-plated sheets of copper. The "Daguerrotype" as it was humbly dubbed by its creator was superceded around 1885 when the American inventor George Eastman managed to create a portable camera that could transfer an image onto celluloid film. Of course this remarkable technology was itself superceded and the Eastman Kodak company filed for bankruptcy protection in January 2012, a victim of the digital revolution. When the Lumiere Brothers invented the cinematograph in 1895 pictures suddenly came alive with movement and audiences gasped and screamed, fleeing away from the screen at the strain of registering this new experience. The eye had let light in but it took a while for the soul to catch up with what it all meant. The stage was set for a new era of visual culture that is still with us. Of course the delighting of the eye (and the soul to which it is a window) is an ancient as well as a modern experience. The rich mosaics and tapestries of the ancient world and the kaleidoscopic narratives captured in medieval stained glass delighted the eyes and thus the hearts and imaginations of the ancients just as surely as the cinema has captivated moderns.

According to Robert Webber, in *Ancient Future Faith*, "evangelicals [in particular] must rethink their enmeshment with modernity and construct a theology that will be consistent with historic Christianity yet relevant to our new time and culture...The shift of postmodern communications to the power of symbolic communication is a call to return to the classical period when the church was an embodied experience of God expressed in life-changing rituals of immersed participation."[17] Seeing is a profoundly spiritual business and faith is something deeply visionary enabling us to look at the world through Jesus' eyes. The Bible is a visionary text that brings into being a wide-eyed people. Just as the camera manipulates light to give us fresh visions, so Christianity is a way of light whose wisdom enchants the imagination, produces spiritual vision and turns us into focused disciples.[18]

Seeing things is not just about a passive reception of stimuli upon the optic nerve. I once insulted the theologian Alister McGrath (a man I greatly admire) by telling him that a good speaker doesn't need a power point presentation. My comment wasn't aimed at *his* presentation but was my attempt to make the point that a good public speaker uses words to create pictures in the minds of the hearers and does not need to rely overly much on lots of dot points projected on a screen. This is why video did not in fact kill the radio star. When we listen to the radio our brains get to create their own pictures rather than the somewhat more passive delivery of ready-made images offered by television and film. We are, it seems, created as image making beings.

All of this has important implications for our planning and practice of worship. "Indications of a postmodern worldview indicate that mystery, with its emphasis on complexity and ambiguity, community, with its emphasis on the interrelationship of all things. And symbolic forms of communication, with an emphasis on the visual, are all central to the new way of thinking."[19] Those who are participating in the kaleidoscopic world of Alt.worship are not attempting to reinvent the Gospel but to plunge deeply into its ages-long roots and live out of those roots in fresh and alive ways.

One of the most positive and encouraging aspects of the Emerging Church movement is its willingness to recover ancient forms of worship that other Evangelicals have forgotten, or reject because they seemed "too Catholic" or "too medieval." Ancient practices such as silent prayer and meditation, the use

---

17   Webber, *Ancient-Future Faith*, 20-24.

18   See Stuart C. Devenish, *Seeing is Believing: The Eye of Faith in a Visual Culture* (Eugene, OR: Wipf & Stock, 2012) for an insightful discussion of the place of the visual in Christian spirituality.

19   Webber, *Ancient-Future Faith*, 35.

of icons and other visual stimuli, illuminating the worship space with candles, and greater appreciation for the power of the sacraments as "visible words" of power, have all been integrated into contemporary worship formats in a rich kaleidoscope of media. The "tent" of the revivalists has been transformed into a "kaleidoscope." This is a reflection of the post-modern concern to be freed from the idea that we can simply recite propositional truths in our worship and this will be enough to convince and convert unbelievers as well as shape the lives of Christians. There is a new confidence in the power of mystery, story, the visual, and the sensual, which is helping to enrich Christian worship in fresh and creative ways.

Given that many people coming into our churches today are going to have what has been described here as a "post-modern" outlook what factors should be considered in planning today's worship?

- Our worship should be participatory, reflecting a web of relationships, not a simple subject-object affair where the pastor talks and everybody else listens. Responsive readings, coming forward for Communion (rather than being served in our seats), the use of dramatic readings, drama, and other performance items help to create this web of creative activity.

- We should use narrative (story) to good effect – story telling is at the root of all human culture. Preaching should not be a series of abstract propositions but filled instead with vivid narratives that "enchant" people. A friend told me that the film *The Fellowship of the Ring* made him want to be a better person. Right there is the power of story.

- We must recover the church's longstanding appropriation of the visual. Unfortunately, because of perceived abuses of the Medieval Church, Protestants have tended to be iconoclastic – because people came to *depend* on pictures Protestants smashed them. We can use new technologies such as Powerpoint (a far better tool for visual than for textual communication) to recover the use of images. We can use sculpture, painting, banners, flowers, colour etc. to appeal to people through the eye-gate. We use the expression "the eyes are the windows to the soul" to refer to something we see in a person's eyes, but the expression can also work in the reverse. People see out through their eyes and their spirits are fed through the visual.

- Discover the other senses as well – remember there are five. The church should not be a drab place but a place of sensual delights. To taste bread and wine, to smell incense, to hear music, other than the usual McWorship choruses, that draws from the rich diversity of world music, to touch each other with a holy handshake, these are all ways that we as a holy people can redeem the sensual from its captivity to the sexual.

Summary

The "auditorium" of the Reformers and the "tent" of the Revivalists underwent considerable change in the "kaleidoscope" of the twentieth and early twenty-first centuries. Popular music replaced classical styles in many Evangelical churches and there was a shift from what is "proper" to what is "relevant." The Sunday morning worship service took on the pattern of an evangelistic meeting for the purpose of winning converts and the historic four-fold pattern was greatly obscured. At the same time the Liturgical renewal that took place in mainline Protestantism drew the church's attention back to earlier liturgies and an appreciation for worship as an engagement with God. Protestant and Catholic liturgies found an unprecedented level of convergence. The Second Vatican Council revolutionised worship patterns in the Roman Catholic Church providing for greater participation of the people. The Charismatic Renewal movement saw experiences that had formerly been confined to Pentecostal sects, such as tongues speaking and prophecy, into the mainstream of Christian life. The wholesale appropriation of popular music forms by Pentecostals has contributed much to their global expansion. The post-modern emphasis on experience, narrative, the visual and the sensual have all had their impact on the Church's worship practices.

Some Questions

1. Which of the contributing influences on worship in the second half of the twentieth century described in this chapter do you see reflected in your own congregation's worship?

2. Would you add other "positives" or "reservations" about Charismatic worship to the list I have given?

3. Do you think your church's worship is most influenced by a "modern" outlook or a "post-modern" one? Explain your answer.

4. How does your congregation use visual stimulation in worship and what "story" elements are present?

5. List at least one way each of the five senses are being or could be engaged in your congregation's current worship practice.

6. How does your congregation listen and respond to God's Word?

Further Reading:

Burns, Stephen. *Pilgrim People: An Invitation to Worship in the Uniting Church.* Adelaide: MediaCom Education, 2012.

Davies, Horton. *Worship and Theology in England Volume 3: The Ecumenical Century 1900-1965, and Crisis and Creativity 1965-Present.* Cambridge: University Press, 1996.

Johansson, Calvin M. *Disciplining Music Ministry: Twenty-first Century Directions.* Peabody: Hendrickson, 1992.

Keifert, Patrick R. *Welcoming the Stranger: A Public Theology of Worship and Evangelism.* Minneapolis: Fortress Press, 1992.

Kimball, Dan. *Emerging Worship: Creating Worship Gatherings for New Generations.* Grand Rapids: Zondervan, 2004.

Lakeland, Paul. *Postmodernity: Christian Identity in a Postmodern Age* Minneapolis: Fortress, 1997.

Spinks, Bryan. *The Worship Mall.* London: SPCK (Alcuin Club), 2010.

CHAPTER NINE

Symbols and Sacraments in Worship

Decoding Signs

Soon after coming to one particular congregation as a new pastor I noticed that the congregation remained standing after the sermon, waiting for me to exit the sanctuary before they would be seated. This was a symbolic action that was new to me and as I tried to "decode" it I realised that there was an interpretive generation gap at work. The older people of the congregation believed that it symbolised standing in respect for the preaching of God's Word, allowing them a few moments of brief reflection upon the sermon before commencing the hubbub of everyday conversation. This was indeed the original intention of the action. The younger people of the church thought it symbolised something different altogether. They thought it was meant to convey the message that the minister was a "big shot" who was more important than the rest of the congregation and before whom "mere mortals" had to remain standing. Clearly the older generation had failed to educate the younger on the meaning of the symbol. Not only had the ritual meaning of the action been lost to the younger people; they had themselves invested it with a new meaning, not part of the original intention.

Those raised in particular denominations use symbols in worship that have very precise inferences, obvious to the insider but perhaps not to the outsider. "Those within the congregation are raised to understand the code words and actions. Those on the outside of that congregation do not decode the word and actions in the same way."[1] Pastors must quickly learn to decode these words and actions before they can be effective in their congregations.

The study of signs and symbols and of their decoding is called "semiotics." This is a complex and interesting field that helps us in understanding the function of symbols in worship. Theology can never describe God in exactly the way that God is, but *symbols* mediate an understanding of God to us. Symbols are in fact a part of everyday life. All of the many ways that we communicate with each other are symbolic and all of the ways that God communicates with us are also signs and symbols of God's presence. From the perspective of communications theory, "all words, actions, facial expressions, sounds, silences, physical arrangements, smells, clothing, hair, length etc. are symbols

---

1   Robert L. Browning and Roy A. Reed, *The Sacraments in Religious Education and Liturgy* (Birmingham, Alabama: Religious Education Press, 1985), 71.

which must be decoded by others. All of us use words, actions, physical arrangements, to encode messages we wish to communicate to others."[2]

Even words themselves are symbols that only *point to* the realities they signify and are not the things themselves. Browning and Reed remind us that "we are never dealing with reality in a final way but always with systems of signs which become codes through which we capture the meaning of our lives and communicate our understandings and feelings about ourselves, others, and ultimate reality."[3] God is "an identified mystery which still remains a mystery."[4] This doesn't mean that we can never understand anything at all about God, but it does remind us that we need symbols to convey to our limited and finite minds what can be known of the infinite God.

The Meaning of Signs and Symbols

Signs indicate meanings we want to convey. They must be precise in order to function properly, and to ensure that we don't make mistakes. A red light means "stop" and if there is any uncertainty about that we are going to have some panel beating bills, if not some funeral expenses. Natural signs such as wet streets indicate that it has rained. Artificial signs include such things as the "slippery when wet" road sign, or the blowing of a whistle or waving of a flag when the train is leaving the station.

We sometimes speak of the bread and wine of Communion as "signs" or "symbols" of Christ's body and blood. Is there any difference between a sign and a symbol? Some theorists have distinguished between signs, which are mere conventions, informational in nature, and symbols which convey meaning at a much deeper level. According to Suzanne Langer, symbols, "are not proxy for their objects, but are vehicles for the conception of objects."[5] As already stated, when we talk about things we have only conceptions of those things, and not the things themselves. It is the conception, stimulated by our imagination and thought, and not the thing itself that a symbol "means." The essence of a religious symbol, according to Paul Tillich, is that it actually participates in the power it symbolises. A symbol "grows organically" and opens up "in two directions – in the direction of reality [the thing symbolised] and in the direction of the mind [how we perceive the thing being symbolized]."[6]

---

2   Browning Reed, 70.

3   Browning and Reed, 72.

4   Edward Schillebeeckx, *The Understanding of Faith: Interpretation and Criticism* (London: Scribner, 1974), 16.

5   Suzanne Langer, *Philosophy in a New Key: A Study in the Symbolism of Reason, Rite, and Art* (Harvard University Press, 1957), 25.

6   Paul Tillich, *Religious Symbolism* (New York: Harper, 1955), 109.

Symbols grow organically out of the life of a community and its experiences. For this reason, they cannot be just arbitrarily invented. Because they are the result of a creative encounter with reality, they die without a connection to that reality. If we were to say tomorrow, "Let's make the switch blade knife the symbol of Christ's death," it would never function well as a symbol because it does not correspond to the reality to which it claims to point. Jesus died on a cross and that historic reality determines the symbol for all time. The outward sign of a symbol must have a close correspondence with the thing being symbolised. We are baptised in water, not in oil, because water is a cleansing element, whereas oil is a healing element.

Protestants must balance their "passion for symbol breaking," often seen as necessary for the reform of the faith, with an understanding of the primal function of symbols, and of their healing and creative religious power. Carl Jung identified a number of recurring primal symbols (or "archetypes") within the human mind that transcend all human religions, cultures and times. These include the hero figure, the child wonder, the cleansing and rebirth of water, the temptress, the evil force, and the saving element, all features often found in myths and stories. Jung rebuked Protestants for demolishing symbols in their worship and F. W. Dillistone believed that if symbols were not used for a good purpose they would be used in destructive ways. "The power of these archetypal images is too great to be rendered null and void by any process of deliberate exclusion. If they are not sanctified within the Christian context they will almost certainly present themselves in demonic forms."[7]

Even the absence of symbols is itself symbolic. The clean, unadorned lines of a Baptist chapel figure the unwillingness to place into physical form a God who can never be circumscribed by humanly constructed art. The silence of a Quaker gathering speaks volumes as a statement about the impotence of human speech in conveying the mystery of God.

The Distinction between Secondary and Core Meanings of Symbols

It is important not to get stuck in the secondary meaning of a religious symbol but to penetrate to its core and primary meaning. The objects of bread and wine were hugely significant in the Roman Mass of the medieval period, but the stress in Catholic theology today is on the action of the faith community when it takes the bread and cup and celebrates its redemption. Sacraments are best understood as events or actions, participated in by the whole community, rather than as "things" to be dispensed to the faithful from the hands of the clergy. There are particular theories about how Christ is present in the Eucharist which may be seen as "secondary" explanations. The "core" meaning

---

7   F. W. Dillistone, *Christianity and Symbolism* (Louisville: Westminster Press, 1955), 187.

is the affirmation that Christ is present to us in Holy Communion even if we cannot explain *how* this is so. The meanings conveyed by symbols are better thought of as 'multivalent', offering up many different meanings to those who participate in them.

Unfortunately, especially in Evangelical and Pentecostal circles, the word "symbol" has come to mean "something not only distinct from reality but in essence even contrary to it…the word 'symbol' ceased to designate something real and became in fact the antithesis of reality."[8] This reduces our use of symbols to the level of object lessons. The typical Lord's Supper service in an Evangelical church can too easily become a mental exercise in remembering something that took place in the distant past rather than the present-tense spiritual experience it is meant to be. The words in the Communion service of the Wesleyan Methodist Church of Australia, drawn from their Anglican precedent, are meant to tie remembrance and experience together, as people are asked not only to "remember that Christ died for you" [the memorial aspect] but also to "feed on him in your heart by faith with thanksgiving" [the participating aspect]. How often have you heard a pastor or other leader at a Communion service say something like, "This is *only* a symbol" or "This is *merely* a symbol"? Worse still they may add to the text of scripture by saying, "Jesus said 'this *represents* my body.'" The words in italics were not spoken by Jesus at all. He simply said, "This *is* my body" leaving the mystery intact. Far from symbols *replacing* reality, they are meant to remind us that the real world – the genuine nature of all creation – is its revelation as the place of God's saving power. Christian symbols tell us that the "real world" is not the world of death, destruction, war, greed, selfishness, and an anticipated global apocalypse. These are aspects of the illusory world because they are temporary. The real world is the world of the kingdom – of salvation, healing, wholeness, redemption and new creation.

> The purpose of a symbol is not to illustrate (this would presume the absence of what is illustrated) but rather to manifest and to communicate what is manifested…The symbol does not so much "resemble" the reality that it symbolizes as it participates in it, and therefore is capable of communicating it in reality.[9]

In the Christian sacraments the empirical (visible) and the spiritual (invisible) are united:

- Not logically (this "stands for" that)

---

8   Alexander Schmemann, *The Eucharist: Sacrament of the Kingdom* (Crestwood, New York: St. Vladimir's Seminary Press, 1988), 30-31.
9   Schmemann, 38.

- Not analogically (this "illustrates" that)
- Not by cause and effect (this "becomes" that)
- But *epiphanically* (this "manifests" that) – one reality manifests and communicates the other.

How can we meaningfully speak of Christ being actually present in a symbol, as we say he is present to us in Holy Communion? Perhaps the contemporary phenomenon of Internet romances helps us here. It is possible to know a person even when that person is physically absent from us. It seems that it is even possible to fall in love with such a person.

> Christ's Eucharistic presence is a personal presence, a type of presence which is humanly much more "real" than mere physical presence. I can be physically present in a room with you; indeed I can be personally present to someone I love even when I am physically absent…People can even make love without being present to each other. At the level of primary symbolism, the kind of presence of which the Eucharist speaks cannot be laid out on a table, any more than you or I nail down and take hold of what makes another personally present to us. Least of all in intimacies like the act of love. We can say a great deal about what personal presence is not, but we can never objectify everything it is.[10]

Jesus died for us two thousand years ago and the "symbols" of his body and blood are *not* meant to tell us, "This is *only* a symbol." Rather they are signs that manifest the reality of his Living Presence among us now.

Defining Sacraments

Understood in a broad sense, a sacrament is any sign given to humanity through ordinary sense objects which reveals sacred things. In the early church, the Latin word *sacramentum* was borrowed from military usage and used by Tertullian (c.100-165) and others, to refer to those badges of profession which mark Christians out as distinct from other persons, and as under a certain obligation, or duty of service, to their Master. It was also the word used by the Latin Fathers, in translating the New Testament word *mysterion* often translated in English as "mystery." It was used in a rather indeterminate sense among the Fathers, as referring to a whole range of things which might set forth "the hidden mysteries of God."[11]

In the writings of St. Augustine of Hippo (354-430 CE) we have a developed theology of the sacraments which forms a definitive reference point for all subsequent thinking on the subject. For Augustine, a sacrament not only

---

10   Tad Guzie, *Jesus and the Eucharist* (Paramus, New Jersey: Paulist-Newman, 1974), 110.
11   Brian Davies, *The Thought of Thomas Aquinas* (Oxford: Clarendon Press, 1992), 347.

shows forth as a sign (*signum*) but also brings about that sacred thing (*res*) that it signifies. "The baptismal water [both] touches the body and cleanses the heart."[12] In his fifth century disputes with the schismatic Donatists, Augustine insisted that it is not the validity of priestly orders that validates the sacrament. Rather, it is the grace conveyed in the sacraments themselves that really matters. Do sacraments convey grace – *ex opere operato* - on account of the sacramental action itself - or *ex opere operantis* - on account of the person giving or receiving the sacramental action? The Donatists said the latter, thus disallowing the power of any sacrament performed by a lapsed presbyter. Augustine said the former, establishing the important theological principal that it is not the character or official standing of the one performing the sacrament that gives it its efficacy but the promise of the grace of God inherent within the sacrament.

Augustine's sacramental theology was reaffirmed by Peter Lombard (c.1096-1164) whose famous Sentences served as a medieval text book in theology, and from which Thomas Aquinas (1225-1274), perhaps the greatest theologian of the Middle Ages, and most of his contemporaries, drew. Aquinas' insistence that truth is communicated to humanity through sense objects lies at the heart of his theology of the sacraments.[13] Medieval theologian numbered the sacraments at seven - Baptism, Confirmation, Eucharist, Penance, Extreme Unction, Marriage, and Orders. Earlier writers had listed many more than this, but by Aquinas' time the Catholic Church had pretty much reached consensus on the number, and it seems not to have been the controversial question until the sixteenth century when the Reformers reduced the number to two – Baptism and Eucharist. It should be kept in mind however that Catholic and Orthodox Christians who affirm seven sacraments, still give a certain primacy to the two core sacraments of Baptism and Eucharist, and Protestants perform each of the other five, in some form or other and believe them to have a certain sacramental quality to them even if they are not strictly speaking designated as sacraments.

Aquinas laid out the manner in which each of the seven sacraments is necessary for the perfection of the believer. Five relate to the believer's perfection as an individual and two to the perfection of his communal life. Baptism is the washing of regeneration, which enables a person to begin the Christian life. Confirmation provides the strength supplied by the Holy Spirit, for continuance in the faith. The Eucharist is the sustenance for the long journey. Penance is a way of maintaining health and healing for the soul, and Extreme

---

12   Latin: *Corpus tangit et cor abluit*, cited in Davies, 357.
13   Peter Kreeft, ed. *A Summa of the Summa: The Essential Philosophical Passages of St. Thomas Aquinas' Summa Theologica Edited and Explained for Beginners* (San Francisco: Ignatius Press, 1990), 48, footnote 35.

Unction prepares the soul for the passage out of this life. Then there are the two sacraments which pertain to community. Priestly orders are for "receiving power to rule the community and exercise public acts" and Marriage is for "the natural propagation of the species."[14] In outlining the practical necessity of sacraments Aquinas pointed out that human nature must be led from things sensible to things divine. Because humanity fell bodily it must receive salvation in a bodily manner. Through worship in physical forms, believers are protected against the superstitious idolatry of worshipping unseen things, such as demons and spirits.[15]

The Protestant Reformers also held a very high view of sacramental grace though they often differed sharply from accepted Catholic theology, especially on the Eucharist. In affirming the priority of preaching, some of their followers (though not the Reformers themselves) tended to downgrade the sacraments. There were clearly historical reasons for this, but they are not reasons that need to be binding on us today. While early in his career Martin Luther included Penance as among the sacraments, he came later to reject this, whilst continuing to stress the importance of confession in the Church, reducing the medieval sacraments from seven to two in number - Baptism and Eucharist. In baptism, "a special promise of grace is offered in conjunction with a particular material sign, water...It is the regular means of regeneration or new birth into Christ and thus of incorporation into his body the church; it is therefore normally necessary for salvation."[16] This new birth is given also to infants, and the Augsburg Confession, condemns the Anabaptists "who allow not the Baptism of children and affirm that children are saved without Baptism."[17] In answer to the question, "What is Baptism?" Luther's *Small Catechism* asserts the well-known Lutheran connection, deriving from St. Augustine, between the Word and the Sacrament.

> Baptism is not simply common water, but it is the water comprehended in God's command and connected with God's Word...without the Word of God the water is nothing but water, and no baptism; but with the Word of God it is a baptism - that is a gracious water of life and a washing of regeneration in the Holy Ghost.[18]

---

14   Thomas Aquinas, *Summa Theologica, Latin text and English translation, Introductions, Notes, Appendices and Glossaries*. Volume 56, "The Sacraments," trans. David Bourke (London: Blackfriars,1974), 33.

15   Aquinas, *Summa* 56:37.

16   Robert H. Fischer, "Baptism," in Julius Bodensieck, ed. *The Encyclopedia of the Lutheran Church* (Minneapolis: Augsburg Publishing House, 1965), I:179.

17   "Of Baptism: Article IX of The Augsburg Confession (1530)," in Schaff, *Creeds*, III:13.

18   "Luther's Small Catechism (1529), Part IV:I," in Schaff, *Creeds*, III: 85-6. Luther does not here mean preaching when he speaks of the "Word of God" but rather the baptismal

In response to "the Zwinglian doctors" the *Formula of Concord* (1576) asserted that Lutherans "teach and confess that in the Lord's Supper the body and blood of Christ are truly, substantially present, and that they are truly distributed and taken together with the bread and wine."[19] Article X of the Augsburg Confession and the Small Catechism assert the same doctrine.[20] Ernst Sommerlath, rejects the standard distinction between the Catholic Church as the church of the sacraments and the Protestant Church as the church of the Word, as not corresponding to the facts and asserts that, "[O]ur Lutheran Church could not and would not live without [the sacraments]...A church which does not highly esteem and constantly use Baptism and the Lord's Supper as means of grace, could not qualify as a truly Christian church."[21]

The Nature of Sacramental Faith

James White defines sacraments as "communal events and sign acts through which God gives himself to us."[22] The sacraments primarily speak of God's action among us, rather than our action before God.[23] Yet, modern Christians have too often been in the grip of an "Enlightenment" view of sacraments which sees them as human actions that *we* perform and which help us remember what God has done *in the past*. This Enlightenment approach places stress on things such as self-commitment ("Am I *ready* to take the step of being baptised?"), worthiness and/or unworthiness to receive ("Am I spiritual enough to go forward for communion?"), and proper understanding ("Is she old enough to understand what she is doing?").

In such a context, "participation in the sacraments elicits guilt, doubt, despair, or avoidance from Christians who see the sacraments as simply one more reminder of their continuing confusion, unworthiness, impotency, and unfaithfulness. Such an experience could hardly be labelled a 'means of grace.'"[24] The classical Christian view, however, has seen God as the actor, and we the acted upon. The believer's response is important - vitally important - but it is always a response that comes *after* God's action.

---

formula of Matthew 28:18, which, by the command of Christ, is to be spoken over every baptised person.

19   "The Formula of Concord (1576), VII:I," in Schaff, *Creeds*, III: 137.

20   Schaff, *Creeds*, III:90.

21   Bodensieck, *Encyclopedia of the Lutheran Church*, 1336.

22   James White, *Christian Worship in Transition* (Nashville: Abingdon, 1976), 42-51.

23   Some of the material in this section is drawn from lectures given by Professor Rob Staples on "Sacraments and Sanctity" at Asbury Theological Seminary Nov. 14-16, 1996. It also draws upon Dr. Staples' book *Outward Sign Inward Grace: The Sacraments in Wesleyan Spirituality* (Kansas City: Beacon Hill Press, 1991).

24   William Willimon, *Worship as Pastoral Care* (Nashville: Abingdon, 1979), 150.

A sacramental faith must have a proper understanding of God as mystery. God became flesh in Jesus Christ, but this only deepens the mystery further so that even as God is revealed in the Incarnation, God yet remains as much question as answer. A sacramental faith embraces this core mystery and is conscious of needing to use a corresponding *language about* God. In one sense we humans create language. In another sense, language creates us, because we are shaped by the language world we inhabit. Two basic kinds of speaking and thinking may be identified - *mythos* and *logos*. *Logos* relates to the faculty of reason. It refers to that which can be proven by rational argument and includes such things as logic, analysis, and critical evaluation. *Mythos*, on the other hand refers to the poetic, artistic, and intuitive side of our being. It is not always subject to rational verification, but holds its mystery within itself with its own self-evident convincing power, that does not depend overly much on logical supports.

People generally think and speak in both modes, mixing both *logos* and *mythos* together, effortlessly moving back and forth between the two. The Hebrew word *debar* is the equivalent of the Greek *logos*, and is used in Jewish theology of the cosmic Word written into the very nature of the universe with its understanding that what God has spoken undergirds all human reason and discourse. The Old Testament is also full of the language of *mythos*, of metaphors that exhibit great imaginative powers speaking of God in ways that delight the imagination as much as they stump the intellect! To say that God's hand is stretched out to save does not mean that he has a giant hand, but it is to speak in symbolic language, to speak metaphorically. To say that the earth is God's footstool does not mean that there is a giant foot descending upon the world! Such language is not meant to be taken *literally*, but it is certainly meant to be taken *seriously*. The biblical writers knew that concrete pictures speak more powerfully than abstract concepts. Jesus knew the same – using vivid and expressive picture language in his parables. Sacraments are also part of this *mythos* language. They are "visible words" – parables of the kingdom – apprehended not only with the mind but with the eyes, the hands, the nose, and the taste buds. The New Testament is broad enough to encompass both *logos* and *mythos*. The Word has become an object of vision and touch. God himself took on human form so that Jesus is the outward visible sign of the invisible God. So the incarnation of God in Christ is the final argument for a sacramental view of the world. All churches express this insight to some extent. Even the Salvation Army, though it does not practice the sacraments of Baptism and Eucharist, has a view of the universe as inherently sacramental and has invested its own special rites, such as the signing of the Soldier's

Covenant, infant dedication, and the use of the Mourners Bench and Holiness Table with a sacramental significance.[25]

We have all heard the expression, "a picture is worth a thousand words." The sacraments function as visible words, saying much more than words can say. They both reveal and conceal. They tell us much but not *everything* that might be known. As signs of the mystery of God, they bring forth modesty in us. Any attempt to *fully* explain how the sacraments convey God's grace to us fails because God cannot be subjected fully to our flawed human analysis. The sacraments ought to unsettle us out of our security by reminding us that while God is present to us God is not completely knowable by us.

As Brian Davies points out, most Christians understand the sacraments as necessary to the development of their relationship with Christ. "A relationship of love is not a static thing to be frozen in a moment of time and established by fiat." A human relationship of love is "shown in what [persons do], day in and day out." It has a "physical history" of sharing between two persons. When Christians participate in the sacraments, they "do things comparable with declaring love, making love, talking, eating together, giving each other presents, and celebrating anniversaries. They express their love in concrete, physical terms, which also count as the embodiment of their love, and therefore, the living out of it."[26] In this sense also, the sacraments are necessary, for no marriage relationship could last long without frequent person-to-person interaction on the concrete, and physical level. No marriage grows in a vacuum of abstract thought about marriage, and no Christian grows in a vacuum of abstract metaphysical reflection about God. God and humanity must touch, and they do so in the sacramental life of the Church.

Nine Symbolic Gestures of Worship

In chapter 11 on "Celebrating Special Days and Seasons" we will discuss some of the symbols of the Church Year (such as the symbol of "light" during Advent). Here we will have a brief look at symbolic actions. These are referred to as "Nine Essential Gestures" by Charles D. Hackett, and Don E. Saliers in their book *The Lord Be With You: A Visual Handbook for Presiding in Christian Worship*.[27] Since many churches would not use several of these actions, "essential" is perhaps not the right word. However, whether or not

---

25   For important reflection on the Salvation Army's understanding of sacramentality see Dean Smith, "Breaking Open the Sacraments," *Pipeline* (July 2010: 6-6, 19) and Adam Couchman, "The Neo-Sacramentality of the Salvation Army," unpublished BTh (Honours) thesis, Sydney College of Divinity, 2007.

26   Davies, *The Thought of Thomas Aquinas*, 355-356.

27   Charles D. Hackett, and Don E. Saliers, *The Lord Be With You: A Visual Handbook for Presiding in Christian Worship* (Cleveland, Ohio: OSL Publications, 1990).

we use these in our own worship, a knowledge of their meaning is helpful in understanding them when we observe them being performed among our fellow Christians. Hackett and Saliers note how Protestants in particular have not been strong on liturgical action.

> At the Reformation, liturgical action, a sense of doing worship together, was never fully recovered, and was often replaced by clergy-dominated monologue, punctuated by hymns…Christian liturgy seeks to manifest a more fundamental language than words and gestures. Faithful liturgy requires incarnate language; the visible and the spoken, the word and the gesture work in concert to communicate what God speaks and enacts… Gestures are…a complex language…the context of gestures is also crucial. The words, 'I've taken about all I'm going to take from you' [will take on a different meaning] depending on whether it was spoken to a friend in a swimming pool water fight or to an antagonist in a lawsuit. The reformed liturgies of the twentieth century are based around the assumption that a particular world of relationships will be created in and through their enactment.[28]

- *Receiving* – standing behind the Communion table to receive the gifts of bread and wine brought forward by representatives of the congregation to be consecrated in the Eucharist, and receiving the offerings of the people.
- *Pouring* – From time immemorial the gesture of pouring has been associated with offering, for example the "drink offerings" (libations) of the Old Testament. The principal pourings in worship are:
  - Pouring wine into the Communion chalice.
  - Pouring water into the baptismal font for baptism or for reaffirmation of baptismal vows.

The action should be visible and audible, with dignity, so that all may see and hear what is being done. The same may be said of course of all liturgical gestures.

- *Offering* – to offer a gift establishes a relationship of mutuality and peace. When we offer things to one another, the appropriate gesture is horizontal with eye contact. When offering to God the gesture is vertical, looking toward heaven.
- *Greeting* – greeting signifies that the worship service is about to begin, or that a new phase of it is about to begin (for example in moving from the service of the Word to the service of the Table). The greeting "the

---

28   Hackett and Saliers, 3-4.

Lord be with you" is biblical (used in the Book of Ruth and elsewhere) and is found in the liturgy from as early as 215 CE. We are in fact commanded by Paul to "greet one another with a holy kiss" (Romans 16:16; 1 Peter 5:14). Whilst a kiss may not be the appropriate gesture in every culture, other greetings may include handshakes, hugs, passing of the peace etc. Cultural decorum and tradition will often help determine which actions to use. When greeting the people it is fitting for the leader to hold his or hands out on a horizontal plane in a gesture of welcome and openness. A distinctively Christian greeting such as "The Lord be with you," or "You are welcome in Christ's Name" is far to be preferred to more casual greetings such as "Well, we had better get started now" or "we can't wait any longer for the late comers so let's begin." Such casual utterances detract considerably from the proper sense of dignity and reverence that gathering in Christ's name should bring.

- *Praying* – the early Christians adopted the prayer postures of the Jewish community. They *stood* before God with hands outstretched and away from their bodies (the "orans" position).

   > They stood and spoke with God face to face without the need to abase or cover themselves. This was the posture of the resurrection. The practice of kneeling and/or sitting to pray developed much later as a sense of unworthiness and pervading sin came to dominate liturgical consciousness.[29]

   Standing to pray is also significant in expressing the status of a "freeman" in the Roman world. Slaves were bareheaded but the free wore a head covering, hence the *yamulkah* or *kippah* worn by Jews to this day.

- *Invoking* – calling God's Holy Spirit down to consecrate the elements we present for God's use. (The prayer of consecration over the elements of communion, called the *epiclesis*, is one of the common examples of this type of prayer/action). The hands are extended, palms down, over the elements being consecrated. The same prayer gesture is appropriate in consecrating water for baptism. In the case of persons, it is used with the "laying on of hands" in confirmation, for the sick, and in ordination.

- *Blessing* – to bless a person is to say that they are in good standing with God. There are three appropriate gestures:
   - Both hands raised high over the shoulders.
   - The left hand on the chest and the right hand only extended.
   - The sign of the cross made in the air.

---

29   Hackett and Saliers, 6.

- *Signing* - The sign of the cross as an emblem of Christian identity reaches very far back in the tradition. The third century *Apostolic Tradition of Hippolytus* refers to making 'the sign of [Christ's] Passion' on the forehead as a protection against the devil.[30] It is used today in baptisms, confirmations, healing, the imposition of ashes on Ash Wednesday, in house blessings, etc. When making the sign upon the forehead with oil, ashes, or water, it should be done with the thumb (it's rude to point), in lines about five centimetres long. In some traditions the sign of the cross is made on the body by the worshipper whenever the name of the Trinity is invoked.

- *Reverencing* – As dependent beings it is appropriate that we bow in humility and awe before the eternal God. Bowing comes from the Roman imperial court, where the protocol called for those approaching the sovereign to drop briefly to the right knee, keeping head and back straight. This was retained in Christian worship as a sign of respect to the bishop or to the altar as the location of Christ's sacramental presence. In the "profound bow" the legs are kept straight while the body and head are declined to a very low position. Prostration (lying face down on the ground before the altar) is another form of reverencing and is still in use in Orthodox and Roman Catholic churches. We know such gestures were in use prior to 451 CE as the Council of Chalcedon in that year forbade kneeling or other penitential gestures during the fifty days of Easter. In Evangelical Protestant churches, the most common form of reverencing is kneeling, usually during prayer, and sometimes at the Communion rail.

Being a Perfect Stranger

What follows is the substance of a talk given in my local church during a Friends Service designed to give unchurched visitors an explanation of the various symbols in our sanctuary and the significance of them for Christian worship. It was inspired by the book *How to be a Perfect Stranger*, a quite cleverly titled, "field guide" to what goes on in religious services of all types.[31] I would encourage you to write something like this about your own congregation. It will encourage greater awareness of your worship practices and the way your worship space is utilised.

---

30   *The Apostolic Tradition of Hippolytus* trans. Burton Scott Easton (Cambridge: Cambridge University Press, 1938), 4:37.

31   Stuart M. Matlins, and Arthur J. Magida, eds. *How to Be a Perfect Stranger: A Guide to Etiquette in Other People's Religious Ceremonies* (Skylight Paths Publishing, 1999).

Christian worship is a mystery to many people, and some church services, in terms of the types of rituals that are carried out, are more mysterious than others. Even the simplest of religious services can seem perplexing to a beginner, so I would like to take time to provide a brief guided tour of our worship space and the objects in it which symbolize our various acts of worship. This description is not designed to be prescriptive in any way. It simply records the symbols in use in one particular church at one particular time.

1. **The Bible and the Pulpit** are in a central location.

This reminds us that God has spoken to the world through prophets, and apostles, and of course, through Jesus Christ. What God has spoken and done have been recorded in the pages of the Bible. It was the first book ever printed on a printing press, and the Bible is still today the best selling book in the world. Elevating the pulpit has a very practical purpose acoustically in order to aid the projection of the voice and the visibility of the speaker. But it also has symbolic value because it tells us of the value of the Bible in the life of the Church.

2. **The Baptismal Font** reminds us that in becoming Christians we belong to a new community.

It is situated at the entrance to the church as baptism is a rite of initiation into that community. It speaks of the forgiveness of sins which is at the heart of our faith. The word "Gospel" literally means "good news." God is willing to forgive us and wash us clean in the waters of baptism. This is very good news indeed. Water is one of the most primal of the elements. Both the Bible and science agree that the earth was formed from out of water, and that life began in water. We are all conceived in the watery environment of our mother's wombs, and we come into this world through water. Water is life; without it we die. When a person first becomes a Christian they are baptised in water, either by sprinkling, pouring or full immersion. The children of Christian parents are also presented for baptism, which speaks of two things: a) That children also belong to the Christian community along with adults and b) That children, having been born naturally, and entered a world of sinfulness and brokenness, are offered a second spiritual birth as they grow older and choose to follow Jesus Christ.

3. **The Cup** is a reminder to us of Holy Communion or the Lord's Supper.

Just as water is a primal element so food and drink are the stuff of life which sustains us physically. The night before Jesus was betrayed and was taken off to be crucified he had a last meal with his followers. He took a loaf of bread and said "This is my body which is given for you. Take and eat this in remembrance of me." He then took a cup of wine and said, "This is my blood which is poured out for you and for many for the forgiveness of sins. Drink this is remembrance of me." Ever since that night, Christians have obeyed Jesus' commands and taken bread and wine in order to remember his death for them. Nothing is more fundamental to human belonging and family than eating together. Twice a month (in many churches weekly) we take the bread and the cup to remind us of Jesus' death for us, of his living presence among us, and of the final reconciliation of all things in him.

4. **The Cross** on the wall speaks also of the love that God has shown toward us.

The cross is probably the most universally recognised symbol of Christianity. Ours is a pretty rough-hewn cross, which reminds us of the agony and pain Jesus suffered for us. However the cross is not ultimately a symbol of death but of life. Jesus died, but rose again on the third day, demonstrating that he has power over death. For this reason Protestants have preferred the sign of an empty cross, as a reminder of Christ's victory, but a cross depicting a suffering Christ is also a powerful sign. It reminds us that though the world exhibits violence in its rejection of the light, such violence does not extinguish the love of God in Jesus Christ. In some way that remains a mystery the hatred and violence is absorbed and out of God's suffering comes healing.

5. **The Candle** is a symbol of the light of Christ.

Jesus said both "*I* am the Light of the world" (John 8:12) and "*You* are the light of the world" (Matthew 5:14). In a world of darkness we know that Christ's light will always shine – a beacon of hope in a weary world. A candle is a fragile light, a soft light, with the appearance of being easily extinguished. Even so, the reality of God's love and power in the world seems often to be extinguished. Where was God during the Jewish holocaust? Or during the tsunamis and earthquakes that have swept away and swallowed up so many lives? These are important questions. Yet the resilience of the human spirit and of faith in the most troubled times is a standing testimony to God's presence in the world.

6. **The Offering Bags**.

Since the very beginning of human religious consciousness, men and women have made offerings to God. In agricultural and tribal cultures this was usually a gift of food – crops, fruit, wine, meat. In a monetary culture like ours it is money that is given. But the idea behind the act is the same – a recognition that what we have does not really belong to us but has been given to us by God. To give back to God recognises this gift and disciplines our tendency to spend more on ourselves than we really need. It should be stressed that this is a voluntary offering. Nobody is asked how much they give. Nobody is asked to give more than their conscience dictates. The basic rule is that laid down by the Apostle Paul – "Set aside a little each week in keeping with your income. Each one should give what he has determined in his heart to give, not reluctantly or under compulsion, but willingly, for God loves a cheerful giver" (2 Corinthians 9:7).

7. The Pulpit Cloth (Parament)

The design on the cloth is often changed to match the particular season of the year – Advent leading up to Christmas, Lent leading up to Easter, etc. At the moment the pulpit cloth bears the letters Alpha and Omega. These are the first and last letters of the Greek alphabet. Jesus said, "I am the Alpha and the Omega; the Beginning and the End, the First and the Last" (Revelation 22:13). Our lives begin and end with him. He is the first in our lives and the last in our lives. He is present at life's dawning and will be present with us in death, and even beyond death.

Some Questions

1. Are there, or have there been in the past, any symbolic actions in worship that you find, or have found, difficult to understand? What are they?

2. What do you think of the following definition of a sacrament? "A sacrament is an outward visible sign of an inward spiritual grace." Do you think this is an adequate definition? Why or why not?

3. Roman Catholic and Orthodox Christians have seven sacraments (Baptism, Eucharist, Confession (now often referred to as "Reconciliation"), Confirmation, Marriage, Ordination, and Anointing the Sick. Protestants reduced these to two - Baptism and Eucharist. In what ways do Protestants still perform actions very similar to the other five without calling them "sacraments"?

4. Sometimes I am asked by a student, "Why do we have bread and wine in the Communion service and not something more culturally relevant such as burgers and Coke?" How would you answer this in light of what you have learned about symbols?

5. Which of the "Nine Gestures of Worship" are present in your own church's worship services? Which of them might helpfully be added? Would you encounter any opposition in introducing any of them? What would be the basis of that opposition and how might you resolve the issue if you felt you needed to?

6. What symbolic actions might you have to explain to a visitor to your church?

Further Reading:

Browning Robert L. and Roy A. Reed, *The Sacraments in Religious Education and Liturgy.* Birmingham, Alabama: Religious Education Press, 1985.

Hackett, Charles D. and Don E. Saliers. *The Lord Be With You: A Visual Handbook for Presiding in Christian Worship.* Cleveland, Ohio: OSL Publications, 1990.

Matlins, Stuart M. and Arthur J. Magida, eds. *How to Be a Perfect Stranger: A Guide to Etiquette in Other People's Religious Ceremonies.* Skylight Paths Publishing, 1999.

Moore, Gerard. "Sacramentality: An Australian Perspective," in Stephen Burns and Anita Monro, eds. *Christian Worship in Australia: Inculturating the Liturgical Tradition* (Sydney: St. Paul's 2009), 139-53.

CHAPTER TEN

Visible Words: Baptism and Eucharist

Baptismal Identity

According to the third century writer, Tertullian, Christians are made, not born.[1] In other words, we only become Christlike through a process of spiritual formation. According to William Willimon, "our identity as Christians is not a matter of birthright, natural inclination, or membership in the human race. God has no grandchildren. I may come to the faith 'just as I am' but I will not be in and under the faith until I submit to being remade, done over, disciplined, processed, incorporated, initiated, in short, reborn."[2] The sacrament of baptism is the principal way that this new identity is symbolised and recalling and remembering our baptism strengthens and confirms our Christian identity.

GHW Lampe stresses the centrality of baptism for a Christian's self understanding:

> Since baptism encompasses the whole Christian life, lack of clarity concerning the meaning of baptism leads to uncertainty all along the line…The more the baptized learn to see their whole life in the light of their baptism, the more does their life take on the pattern of life 'in Christ.' It is also of decisive importance to pastoral care to say to a troubled human being, "You are baptized, with all the assurance which this implies."[3]

Martin Luther's theology of baptism provides a solid foundation for Christian identity and assurance. All of life is to be "baptismal in character" so that the believer may experience the perfect freedom of death to sin and rising to new life.[4]

> There are today as many ordinances, as many rites, as many sects, as many votaries, as many anxieties and works, as there are Christians busied with them: and the result is that Christian people forget they have been baptized. Because of the multitude of locusts, caterpillars, and cankerworms, I say, no one is able to remember that he has been baptized or what benefits follow on baptism. We ought, when baptized, to have been like little children, who are not preoccupied with any cares

---

1   Tertullian, *Apologeticus*, xviii.
2   Willimon, *Worship as Pastoral Care*, 147.
3   G.H.W. Lampe, *One Lord, One Baptism* (1960), 70.
4   Luther, "The Pagan Servitude," 302

or any works, but entirely free, redeemed and safe merely through the glory of their baptism.[5]

In the New Testament there is little distinction made between the church's missionary task and its baptising task – the two go hand in hand. Throughout the Book of Acts, to be converted and to be baptised are one and the same (Acts 8:12, 35; 9:18; 18:8). Paul assumes that all Christians are baptized (1 Cor. 1:11-17). Matthew records Jesus' great commission in terms of baptising converts (Matt 28:18-20).

There are three major areas of disagreement amongst Christians regarding the practice of baptism. The first is a disagreement as to who should be the proper subjects of baptism. The second is a dispute as to the proper mode of baptism. The third is a differing over the expected effects of baptism. Considerably more space will be given to the issue of the proper subjects of baptism, as the others to a great extent rise out of this first consideration. This discussion is not a detour from our study of worship. Since worship is grounded in our baptismal identity, a theological foundation to baptismal practice is a necessary asset.

The Subjects of Baptism

Most Christian churches provide for the baptism of infants, as well as for the baptism of mature age converts.[6] Roman Catholic and Eastern Orthodox churches, Anglicans, Lutherans, Presbyterians and Methodists all baptise infants. Some baptise only the children of believing parents, others are less discriminating. The Baptists, Churches of Christ and Pentecostals do not practice infant baptism, sharing the convictions of the sixteenth century Anabaptists that baptism is only for those who have made a conscious decision to follow Christ. Most are not as confronting as Menno Simons who declared in the sixteenth century that "All [those who baptise infants] should know that their infant baptism does not only not cleanse and sanctify, but that it is altogether idolatry, without promise, pernicious, and contrary to the Word of the Lord."[7] Traditionally membership in a Baptist congregation has depended upon a person having been baptised as a believer by full immersion. Where Baptists have been more ecumenically engaged there has sometimes been a willingness to accept members who have been baptised elsewhere as infants.

The Baptist theologian Augustus H. Strong, defines baptism as "the immersion of a believer in water, in token of his previous entrance into the communion of

---

5   Luther, "The Pagan Servitude," 307.

6   For a concise summary of the rationale for infant baptism see Michael Green. *Baptism: Its Purpose, Practice and Power* (London: Hodder and Stoughton, 1987), 65-77.

7   Menno Simons, 'Concerning Baptism,' http://www.mennosimons.net/ft009-baptism.html accessed 1 May 2013.

Christ's death and resurrection."[8] There are several elements to this definition, which effectively define the Baptist position. Baptism is to be by immersion. It is only to be administered to those who have had a previous conscious experience of salvation. It is symbolic in nature ("a token"). It may be helpful to deal with some of the biblical texts which are often cited in support of the Baptist position, showing the manner in which other Christians have dealt with the same texts.

At the conclusion of Peter's great Pentecost sermon, the crowd was pierced to the heart and cried out, "Brothers, what should we do?" to which Peter replied, "Repent and be baptized each one of you in the name of Jesus Christ so that your sins may be forgiven, and you will receive the gift of the Holy Spirit." (Acts 2:37-38) Here is a call to be baptised in response to an adult hearing of the gospel. It is clearly a decisive act, signifying one's belief in Christ and willingness to follow him. Baptism cannot be of any use to infants since they can neither understand nor intelligently respond to the gospel.

However, paedobaptists (those who baptise infants), point to verse 39 as evidence that the children of those who responded on that day were also included in the covenantal union. "For the promise is for you and your children, and for all who are far off, everyone whom the Lord our God calls to him." (Acts 2:39) In support of this interpretation is the considerable weight of evidence which points to the practice of infant baptism in the case of proselytes to the Jewish faith, during the New Testament period.[9] There is no reason to expect these early Jewish Christians to have departed from the established practice of the day. On the other hand, some more recent scholarship has challenged these earlier views and holds that there is no clear evidence of Jewish proselyte baptism until after 70 CE.[10]

Baptists point to Christ's Great Commission as further indication of the unsuitability of infant baptism. "Go therefore and make disciples of all nations, baptizing them in the name of the Father and of the Son and of the Holy Spirit, and teaching them to obey everything that I have commanded you." (Matthew 28:19-20) How can infants be discipled and taught to be obedient? This must refer, say the Baptists, only to adult believers. However, the above evidence, regarding proselyte baptism, should be kept in mind at this point also. The

---

8   Augustus Hopkins Strong. *Systematic Theology: A Compendium Designed for the Use of Theological Students* (Valley Forge: The Judson Press, 1963), 931.

9   Madsen cites Schurer, Von Soden, Mosheim, Lightfoot and Edersheim as scholars who have argued for such a position. A Madsen. *The Question of Baptism: A Handbook on Infant Baptism* (Melbourne: Spectator, 1912), 31-34.

10   See for example, Scott McKnight, *A Light among the Gentiles* (Minneapolis: Fortress, 1991).

Apostles, upon hearing this command, may well have understood it to imply the baptism of convert's children.

Further evidence of the "proselyte" form of baptism having been retained in the early church may be found in the "household" passages in the Book of Acts. When the Lord "opened the heart" of Lydia to respond to the gospel, "she *and her household* (were) baptized."[11] (Acts 16:14-15) Similarly, in the case of the converted jailer at Philippi, in a cry much like that already referred to on the Day of Pentecost, the jailer cried, "Sirs, what must I do to be saved?" Paul and Silas replied, "Believe on the Lord Jesus, and you shall be saved, you *and your household*...then he *and his entire family were* baptised without delay."[12] (Acts 16:30-33) The Greek word translated in the NRSV "entire family" (*oikos*) refers to the whole family living under the same roof, including the extended family of servants. It is possible, perhaps even likely, that among these there were some infants.[13]

Another passage cited in defence of believers-only baptism is taken from Mark's version of the Great Commission: "The one who believes and is baptised will be saved; but the one who does not believe will be condemned."[14] There is a significant textual problem involved here, however, as these verses (9-20) are not usually considered to be an original part of Mark's gospel. The words are out of keeping with the rest of the tone of scripture in that they seem to make baptism an absolute prerequisite to salvation. It is probably not wise to place too much theological weight on this text.

Paedobaptists make use of Paul's identification of baptism with circumcision in support of their claim that just as circumcision was a sign that children were included in the community of God under the Old Covenant, even so, baptism is a sign of their inclusion in the New Covenant community of faith.[15] They also point to Jesus' words in Matthew 19:14 which describe the kingdom of God as belonging to children. If children are the heirs of the kingdom, how then can they be denied the initiatory ordinance of that kingdom?

It is often claimed that infant baptism is a late invention of the church, evidence of decay in spirituality and sound doctrine following on from Constantine's conversion to Christianity and the resultant secularisation of the church. This

---

11   Italics mine.

12   Italics mine.

13   Bengel says, *quis credit in tot families nullum fuisse infantem*? Roughly translated, "Is it possible that in these families there were no infants?" Cited by R.J. Knowling in W. Robertson Nicoll, *The Expositor's Great Testament*. Volume II (Grand Rapids: Wm. B. Eerdmans Pub. Co., 1988), 346.

14   Mark 16:16 (NASB)

15   Colossians 2:11-12 (NASB)

is something of a simplistic overstatement. The Didache (c.100 CE.) mentions the practice of infant baptism, as does Irenaeus (c.130-202). Origen (c.185-254) claims that "the Church has received a tradition from the Apostles to give baptism to little children."[16] Cyprian, in the second century, argued that infants should be baptised as soon as they are born.[17] Tertullian (c.160-220) opposed the practice, perhaps under the influence of the Montanists. His very opposition, however, gives evidence of its use in the church from the earliest times.

The Reformed tradition often stresses the covenantal nature of baptism as well as the continuity between the 'church in the wilderness' (the Old Testament community of faith) and today's church. Just as the old covenant community had a sign of belonging to the covenant community (circumcision) so the New Testament community has a sign of belonging in the baptismal rite. Those in the Wesleyan theological tradition also find support for the practice of infant baptism, in their theological conviction regarding universal atonement (that Christ died for all people) and prevenient grace (that God's grace is available to all people).

> Since children are born into this world with natures inclined to sin, and yet the prevenient grace of God provides for their redemption during the period before reaching the age of accountability, those parents who so choose may testify to their faith in God's provision by presenting their small children for baptism, while those who prefer to emphasise baptism as a testimony by the individual believer to his [or her] own act of faith may present their children for dedication.[18]

Those churches which do not practice infant baptism still recognise the importance of welcoming the children of believers into the world. However, the focus in a dedication service is more upon the parents and the vows that they are making than upon the child as the recipient of God's grace. It serves a valuable purpose for those churches that reject infant baptism in welcoming the child into the community and reminding parents of their responsibilities. It must be conceded however that infant dedication is not a sacrament but a ritual designed to replace one.

---

16   Cited in Madsen, 90.
17   Alexander Roberts & James Donaldson (eds). *The Ante-Nicene Fathers.* Translations of the Writings of the Fathers down to A.D. 325. Vol V. Hippolytus, Cyprian, Caius, Novatian, Appendix. (Grand Rapids: Wm. B. Eerdmans Pub. Co., 1975), 353.
18   *Wesleyan Handbook,* 150.

John Wesley's *Treatise on Baptism* declared:

> It is not only lawful and innocent, but meet, right, and our bounden duty, in conformity to the uninterrupted practice of the whole Church of Christ from the earliest ages, to consecrate our children to God by baptism, as the Jewish Church were commanded to do by circumcision.[19]

John Wesley provided a doctrinal standard for the American Methodists by abridging the 39 Articles and commending them to the newly emerging Methodist Episcopal Church in America. These 25 Articles provide an important link with Reformation theology and include the above article as well as the statement that "The baptism of young children is to be retained in the Church."[20] The following excerpt from the *Methodist Book of Laws*, demonstrates just how seriously that branch of the Christian church has viewed the obligation of parents to bring their children for baptism.

> All children, by virtue of the Universal Atonement of Christ, are members of the Kingdom of God, and are entitled to be received into the visible Church of Christ at baptism. Parents cannot neglect to present their children to the Lord in baptism without evidently disregarding the appointment of God, and depriving their offspring of a most valuable privilege.[21]

The Wesleyan-Holiness movement developed along somewhat different lines, developing a pluralistic approach to baptism.[22] Believers were allowed to exercise their conscience on the issue of infant baptism and (as we shall see later) on the question as to the mode of baptism. The Wesleyan Methodist Church of Australia still allows for the baptism of infants, though with the disclaimer that such baptism does not replace the need for personal conversion and with the provision that only the children of *believers* should receive the sacrament.[23] The same pluralistic approach is also evidenced by the inclusion, in the *Beacon Dictionary of Theology*, of two articles on "infant Baptism" – one "Pro" the other "Con."[24]

---

19   John Wesley, "A Treatise on Baptism," cited in Albert Outler, ed. *John Wesley* (New York Oxford University Press, 1964), 331.

20   See Thomas C. Oden. *Doctrinal Standards in the Wesleyan Tradition* (Grand Rapids: Francis Asbury Press of Zondervan, 1988,) pp.99-126 for a comprehensive treatment of Wesley's abridgement of the 39 Articles.

21   *The Methodist Book of Laws,* 1908. Cited in Madsen, ii.

22   See Stan Ingersol, "Christian Baptism and the Early Nazarenes: The Sources that Shaped a Pluralistic Baptismal Tradition" in *Wesleyan Theological Journal* (Volume 25, No.2 Fall 1990).

23   *The Discipline of the Wesleyan Church* (Indianapolis: Wesleyan Publishing House, 1984).

24   Richard S. Taylor (ed). *Beacon Dictionary of Theology* (Kansas City: Beacon Hill Press of Kansas City, 1983), 280-81.

It is not my intention to argue here for one or other position on infant baptism, though my preference may be discernable. Readers will make the relevant applications to their own worship context. I certainly want to heed the warning of John Calvin that "that those who raise controversies and contentions on the subject of infant baptism are presumptuous disturbers of the Church of Christ."[25] The Baptist emphasis is valuable in placing a focus upon the candidate's profession of faith and public declaration of Christ's Lordship. These are surely important aspects of baptismal practice. Those who practice infant baptism prefer to stress the objective nature of the sacrament as ordained by God and as bringing God's promise to the believer before the person's conscious response, thus emphasising the priority of grace. It is possible to take a "both/and" rather than an "either/or" approach.

The Mode of Baptism

As to the mode of baptism, Christians admit a variety of practices. The Greek word translated "baptise" means "to dip" or "to plunge," which seems to suggest immersion. However, the word has a wider use, and may include the idea of wetting, washing and cleansing. Romans 6:3-4 and Col. 2:12 are sometimes taken as conclusive arguments for immersion, since sprinkling or pouring cannot symbolise the believer's identification with Christ's death and resurrection. But it is clear that the biblical writers use several other images in their explanation of the meaning of baptism. In 1 Corinthians 10:1-4, baptism speaks of a new allegiance. Just as the Israelites were "baptized into Moses in the cloud and in the sea," so believers have been baptised into Christ. 1 Peter 3:20-22 places the emphasis on the inward nature of baptism, "not as the removal of dirt from the body, but as an appeal to God for a good conscience." It is difficult to find a single central meaning of baptism in Scripture but cleansing and incorporation are equally as present as death and resurrection. Such meanings may be symbolised quite adequately by full immersion, but may be equally well represented by sprinkling or pouring.

Thomas Aquinas conceded that there were many benefits to baptism by full immersion, but did not insist on this particular mode. "Even though it is safer to baptize by immersion, because this is the more common usage, baptism can be conferred by sprinkling or pouring on water."[26] Pouring began in the Roman Catholic Church in the twelfth century, but Aquinas' statements seem to indicate that immersion was the most commonly employed mode in his day.[27] In cases of large numbers of candidates for baptism, or scarcity of water,

---

25   Cited in Paul K. Jewett, *Infant Baptism and the Covenant of Grace* (Grand Rapids: Eerdmans, 1978), frontispiece.

26   Aquinas, *Summa*, 57:31.

27   Immersion would disappear from Catholic use after the sixteenth century (but

or feebleness of the minister or the person being baptized, immersion would be ill advised, and another mode can be used without in any way invalidating the sacrament. Whatever is an accident of baptism, such as the amount of water used, does not change the substance of baptism. Triple immersion may be performed, and in fact seems to have been the usual practice in Aquinas' day, but again this was not considered necessary, but accidental only.

Martin Luther accepted the traditional Augustinian view that baptism brings a washing away of sin but did not see this as expressing the full significance of the rite believing that burial and resurrection more fully expresses what takes place in the rite. "A sinner requires not so much to be washed, as to die. This is in order that he should be reborn and made another creature, and that the rite may correspond with the death and resurrection of Christ."[28] For this reason, Luther favoured full immersion in baptism (though Lutherans have not generally followed this practice.) This dying and rising is not a once-off affair. The ceremony itself lasts only a short time but that which it signifies lasts throughout life, "i.e. every day we die and every day we rise again."[29]

We saw earlier that churches in the Wesleyan-Holiness tradition take a pluralist approach to the question of whether to baptise infants or only believers. Those same churches take a similar approach in regard to the mode of baptism. Candidates may be baptised by immersion, sprinkling, or pouring.[30] To some, this represents a non-committal approach to an important area of truth. Should one not fall down on either side of the fence with more definiteness and precision? However, the strength of this position should not be overlooked. It allows liberty of conscience as well as flexibility in practice. Furthermore it places the emphasis where it needs to be – on the saving and sanctifying grace of God that is not hindered by the precise mode that is used or the amount of water that is expended.

The Reformed theologian Louis Berkhof cites a series of biblical texts in support of the idea that baptism symbolises spiritual cleansing and purification.[31] He goes on to quote Question 69 of the Heidelberg Catechism:

---

not in the Eastern Orthodox churches, where it is still used, even for infant baptism). The Roman rite has recently been revised so as to recommend immersion, including in the case of children, because of its powerful symbolism. Aquinas, *Summa*, 57: 30-31, footnote.

28   Martin Luther, "The Pagan Servitude of the Church" [usually referred to as "The Babylonian Captivity of the Church"] in John Dillenberger, ed. *Martin Luther: Selections from His Writings* (New York: Doubleday, 1962), 302.

29   Luther, "Pagan Servitude," 302.

30   Wesleyan Methodist Church of Australia *Handbook*, para 150.

31   Acts 2:39; 22:16; Romans 6:4f; 1 Corinthians 6:1; Titus 3:5; Hebrews 10:22; 1 Peter 3:21 and Revelation 1:5.

Q: How is it signified and sealed unto you in holy baptism that you have a part in the sacrifice of Christ on the cross?

A: Thus, that Christ has appointed the outward washing with water and added the promise that I am washed with His blood and Spirit from the pollution of my soul, that is, from all my sins, as certainly as I am washed outwardly with water, by which the filthiness of the body is commonly washed away.[32]

The quantity of water used is secondary to the inward sanctifying work that God effects in the recipient. In the case of adults this work is immediate and actual. In the case of infant baptism, grace is offered in the form of a promise or pledge, the efficacy of which depends upon subsequent conscious appropriation.

The Effects of Baptism

Another consideration is the effect of baptism. Precisely what does baptism *do* for the recipient? Again there are three major views. Roman Catholics, Orthodox Christians and mainstream Protestants consider the sacrament of baptism to be a means of grace, though there are differences between different traditions on precisely *how* this is so. Baptist and Pentecostal churches are among those who see baptism as symbolic of a commitment already made by the believer and as an act of obedience. It does not convey grace in any special sense (though God is certainly believed to be present to bless the ceremony), but is the believer's public declaration of Christ's Lordship and an initiation into a local community of fellow believers. There is a nice balance of the human and divine elements in baptism in Article 27 of the 39 Articles of the Anglican Church.

Baptism is not only the sign of profession and mark of difference whereby Christian men are discerned from others that are not christened, but is also a sign of Regeneration or new birth whereby *as by an instrument, they that receive baptism rightly* are grafted into the Church; the promises of forgiveness of sin and of our adoption to be sons of God by the Holy Ghost are visibly signed and sealed.[33]

In the words of Michael Green, "(Baptism) is an instrument…if you receive it aright…Baptism puts you into Christ, if you let yourself be put."[34]

Some Practical Baptismal Considerations

After God's action the burden of responsibility is with the baptisers (the Church) rather than with the baptised (the believer). It is the church that is

---

32   Louis Berkhof. *Systematic Theology* (London: The Banner of Truth Trust, 1969), 628.

33   Cited in Green, 56.

34   Green, 57.

commanded to baptise and make disciples. It is the church that is to carry out the work of discipleship. Perhaps our tendency to place the burden on the one being baptised is a reflection of our unwillingness or unreadiness to be the kind of community that can make all the promises in baptism effective in the lives of individuals. So, when a person doesn't "make good" on their baptismal vows, we focus on their lack of proper commitment instead of our lack of proper preparation and/or follow up. Or when a person baptised as an infant does not grow up to be a Christian, we focus on the infant's lack of ability to hear and respond to the gospel instead of on the church's failure to nurture the child and the parents in the faith. So the Church must think very carefully about what it is doing in baptism.

- **Place baptism in the context of worship**

  Many people like to go out into the open and baptise, beyond the church's worship space, thinking that this fulfils the requirement that baptism be a "public witness" to faith. While there is certainly nothing wrong with this, there is a strong case for baptism taking place in the course of the church's regular worship life. Baptism speaks of entry to the community of faith, so it is appropriate that it take place in the midst of the worshipping community.

- **Engage in pre-baptismal instruction**

  Though baptisms such as those in the Book of Acts were not always accompanied by careful instruction, it is important that we make such instruction available today. Those who were responding to the Gospel in the New Testament period were usually Jews, proselytes, and God-fearers with a well-established religious knowledge. People do not always have such understanding today. Even the Ethiopian eunuch who had the scriptures available to him, still needed Philip to explain those scriptures more fully before he was baptized (Acts 8:26-39).

  The most ancient method of providing this preparatory instruction through the catechumenate is undergoing a welcome resurgence at the present time as witnessed by the Catholic Church's *Rite of Christian Initiation of Adults*. A person preparing for baptism is sponsored by members of the congregation and encouraged to participate in Christian worship while simultaneously receiving instruction on Christian beliefs and behaviours. This takes place over a period of time which will vary according to circumstances, but provides an opportunity for the person to think deeply through the implications of receiving Christian baptism. In an increasingly secularised world, one can no longer presuppose that a person has received infant baptism and the benefit of a Sunday School education needing now only the act of confirming an already existing faith. Rather, people are often coming from an entirely pagan context and are in need of a more thorough initiation process much like that provided in the earlier centuries of the church.

- **Use a lot of water**

As discussed above, the baptism of believers is often done by full immersion. However, even when using the mode of pouring it's good to allow the properties of the water – its look, feel, and sound, to be clearly experienced by the whole congregation. One way to do this is to pour water from a container into the baptismal font or bowl from a slight height, thus dramatizing the flow of the water, and the promise of the Spirit being "poured out."

- **Use the Apostles' Creed**

The creeds actually began as part of the Church's baptismal rite and then over time became more and more elaborate. To recite the Creed is to remind the one being baptised as well as all in the congregation of the faith into which the person is being baptised. This is not just a nice little experience the person is having but initiation into a community that believes certain things about what God has done in Christ.

- **Ensure the participation of the sponsoring congregation**

Baptism is never a private affair. Willimon tells of a seven year old who swaggered up to the preacher after a baptism and asked, "Where is this baby that belongs to me now? If I'm going to be looking out for him I've got to know exactly what he looks like!"[35] That child had a good understanding of the community's responsibility to nurture all whom it baptises.

- **Lead the congregation in a remembrance of its own baptism**

The minister might, for example, invite any who would like, to come forward and have water sprinkled on them as he or she repeats the simple words, "Remember your baptism and be thankful." This provides an opportunity for a reaffirmation of earlier baptismal vows. Some churches will sprinkle the entire congregation at such times by processing up the aisle while waving a water soaked branch out along the pews giving everyone a little splash as a baptismal reminder. This is the purpose also of the Roman Catholic practice of making the sign of the cross after dipping the figure in water at the entrance to the church – it is an assertion of baptismal identity.

---

35   Willimon, 158.

- **Place baptism in the flow of the church year**

  Traditionally Easter is the preferred time of year though in Australia many people are away on holidays at this time; some Evangelical churches even schedule their church camp over the Easter weekend! There are however other places in the church year that would be appropriate for baptisms including the day of Pentecost and the season of Epiphany. If you know that you are going to have an annual celebration of Baptism you will be better able to prepare people to receive the sacrament through an annual cycle of catechesis.

- **Stress baptism's life-long significance**

  According to Martin Luther, baptism "signifies that the old Adam in us, together with all sins and evil lusts, should be drowned by daily sorrow and repentance and be put to death, and that the new man should come forth daily and rise up, cleansed and righteous, to live forever in God's presence."[36] The old Adam is drowned in baptism but as Luther says elsewhere, "He's a mighty good swimmer." It is not enough just to receive the sacrament as though that settled everything once and for all time. Baptism is only the beginning of a life of discipleship.

Calvin on the Eucharist

Holy Communion is also called simply "Communion," "the Lord's Supper," "the Lord's Table," or "the Eucharist" (from the Greek word meaning "thanksgiving"). The Bible gives no technical explanation of this meal. The church has often been divided over the precise nature of the Eucharist, and there is an irony in this (not to mention tragedy) in that Christ's Table, meant to be a place of hospitality, has often been a cause of rejection and exclusion.

When we come to the Supper of the Lord, our primary focus should not be on precise theological definition but on worship. John Calvin saw Eucharistic communion with Christ as something "I rather experience than understand... In his Sacred Super he bids me take, eat, and drink his blood under the symbols of bread and wine. I do not doubt that he himself truly presents them, and that I receive them...They who are carried beyond this by their own exaggerations do nothing but obscure simple and plain truth with such involvements."[37] While the New Testament teaches that believers should examine themselves before they partake (1 Cor. 11:28) this should not be used to torture and harass "pitiable consciences in dire ways."[38] Being in a state of grace is not to be determined by one's performance, for who is worthy of themselves? It is

---

36   Martin Luther's *Small Catechism* IV:12.

37   Calvin, *Institutes*, IV: 17:32.

38   Calvin, *Institutes*, IV:17:40-41.

faith and love which is requisite, not perfection. "[L]et us remember that this sacred feast is medicine for the sick, solace for sinners, alms to the poor; but would bring no benefit to the healthy, righteous and rich - if such could be found."[39] The worthiness God looks for in us is no more than faith in God's mercy and a loving response to that mercy.

Calvin also argued for a frequent celebration of the Lord's Supper viewing the usual custom of once a year as unsatisfactory. He appealed to the practice of the early church never to meet without partaking of the Supper. He cites the ancient canons of Anacletus and Calixtus, the Apostolic Canons, the Council of Antioch (341) and the First Council of Toledo (400) to prove that believers should not deliberately absent themselves from the Eucharistic celebration. Pope Zephyrinus (198-217) had made a decree that all Christian people should confess their faith at least once a year. Later this was distorted into only insisting on Holy Communion once a year. "By this it has come about," says Calvin, "that almost all when they have taken communion once, as though they have beautifully done their duty for the rest of the year, go about unconcerned." Instead of this "all like hungry men should flock [regularly] to such a bounteous feast."[40]

In regard to the precise manner in which the Supper should be partaken, Calvin allowed quite some latitude - "whether or not the believers take it in their hands, or divide it among themselves, or severally eat what has been given to each; whether they hand the cup back to the deacon or give it to the next person; whether the bread is leavened or unleavened; the wine red or white - it makes no difference. These things are indifferent and left at the church's discretion."[41] He argued for a weekly communion service with the following liturgical elements:

1. Public prayers.

2. Sermon.

3. Bread and wine placed on the table

4. The minister repeats the words of institution ("This is my body; This is my blood")

5. The minister recites the promises connected with the Eucharist, and "excommunicate[s] all who are debarred from it by the Lord's prohibition."

6. Prayer is offered to the Lord that the people would receive with faith and thanksgiving.

---

39   Calvin, *Institutes*, IV:17:42.

40   Calvin, *Institutes*, IV:17:45-46

41   Calvin, *Institutes*, IV:17:43.

7. Psalms are said or sung as the people are given the bread and cup.

8. After the supper there is "an exhortation to sincere faith and confession of faith, to love and behaviour worthy of Christians."

9. Finally thanks should be given, praises sung to God, and the church dismissed in peace.[42]

The Meanings of the Eucharist

It is better to think in terms of the meanings (plural) rather than one single meaning to the Eucharist. Nazarene theologian, Rob Staples lists seven meanings.

- **Celebration** (*eucharistein* - "**to be thankful**').

  There ought to be a note of joyful celebration, rather than of a funeral procession, in Communion. It is after all the *Lord's* Supper, not the *Last* Supper. There may be times such as during Lent when it would be appropriate for the Communion serviced to be marked by a very solemn and penitential atmosphere. But generally speaking, while the Lord's Supper should certainly be reverent, it need not be gloomy. Eucharist is more "fiesta" than "funeral."

- **Commemoration** (*anamnesis*) - "**Do this in remembrance of me.**"

  Here is where we look back to what Christ has done for us on the cross. Even Zwingli, the Reformer who is often credited with the view that the Eucharist is "only" a symbolic exercise in remembrance, recognized that in such remembering, the living Presence of Christ is in the midst of the worshipping Christian community. In 1999 Albert Einstein was voted the Person of the [Twentieth] Century by *Time* magazine because of his profound theories in physics, such as the theory of relativity, which have had vast implications in virtually every field of scientific endeavour. One of the ideas Einstein toyed with was that there may occur at certain times a fold or crinkle in time when events separated by time and space as we currently experience them, could be folded in on themselves so that past, present, and future could be experienced simultaneously. While that sounds like science fiction, the Lord's Supper is, spiritually speaking, something quite like that as it looks backward, forwards, and to the present at precisely the same time. All tenses come together, as we remember his death for us in the past, his living presence with us in the present, and his coming again as a future event.

- **Presentation** (or "**sacrifice**").

  The sacrificial image has occasioned much controversy. The Reformation debate over the Lord's Supper was locked into a restricted view of the

---

42   Calvin, *Institutes*, IV:17:43.

meaning of sacrifice. Medieval thought asserted that each Mass was a renewed sacrifice of Christ. Recent thought gives us a clearer view of the meaning of sacrifice. Reformers stressed our sacrifice of praise and of our whole selves (see Rom. 12:1, 1 Peter 2:5 and Heb. 13:15-16). Charles Wesley's Eucharistic hymns are full of sacrificial language.

> Victim Divine, Thy grace we claim,
> While thus Thy precious death we show:
> Once offered up a spotless Lamb,
> In Thy great temple here below,
> Thou didst for all mankind atone,
> And standest now before the throne.
>
> Thou standest in the holy place,
> As now for guilty sinners slain;
> The blood of sprinkling speaks, and prays,
> All prevalent for helpless man;
> Thy blood is still our ransom found,
> And speaks salvation all around.
>
> The smoke of Thy atonement here
> Darkened the sun, and rent the veil,
> Made the new way to Heaven appear,
> And showed the great Invisible;
> Well pleased in Thee, our God looked down,
> And calls His rebels to a crown.
>
> He still respects Thy sacrifice;
> Its savour sweet doth always please:
> The offering smokes through earth and skies,
> Diffusing life, and joy, and peace;
> To these, Thy lower courts, it comes,
> And fills them with divine perfumes.
>
> We need not now go up to Heaven,
> To bring the long sought Saviour down;
> Thou art to all already given,
> Thou dost e'en now Thy banquet crown:
> To every faithful soul appear,
> And show Thy real presence here![43]

---

43   John and Charles Wesley, Hymn 116 in *Hymns on the Lord's Supper* (Bristol: Farley, 1745), 98-99.

- **Participation** *(koinonia)* – "fellowship, sharing, communion."

  Paul asks the rhetorical questions in 1 Corinthians 10:16, "The cup of blessing that we bless, is it not a sharing in the blood of Christ? The bread that we break, is it not a sharing in the body of Christ?" The word translated "sharing" is *koinonia* and may also be translated "fellowship," "participation," and "communion." When Paul exhorts examination of the heart before taking Communion, in 1 Corinthians 11:17-34, it is in the context of establishing order. To "eat unworthily" means to violate *koinonia*. The "recognition of the body" has both Christological dimensions (in that it is a failure to recognize Christ's presence in the assembly) and ecclesiastical dimensions (in that it fails to give proper regard to fellow Christians as members together of the Body of Christ).

- **Evangelisation**

  Many churches restrict participation in the Communion service only to those who are clearly converted or formally members of their church. John Wesley believed the Lord's Supper was not only a *confirming* but also a *converting* ordinance. (His own mother was brought to full assurance at Communion). He welcomed "penitents" (what we today might call "seekers") to come to the Table and thus take a step closer to saving faith. The only qualification for membership in a Methodist Society was a "desire to flee from the wrath to come" and "be saved from one's sins." This indicates that those coming to the Lord's Table among the Methodists, while they did not need to be fully committed believers, must at least be committed to seeking salvation with all earnestness.

  The practice of an "open table" is a contentious one among Methodists today and a difficult stance to take in an ecumenical context where baptism is normally seen as the rite of entry to the Table, in keeping with the practice of the ancient church. Those who argue for an open table on the basis that Jesus "ate with sinners" (and this is, after all, his Table, not ours), do have a persuasive point. The argument from Wesley's practice of inviting people who had not undergone a conversion experience to approach the Table is less persuasive. It is often forgotten that those Wesley addressed were for the most part baptised as infants and could therefore be admitted to the Table as a way of confirming the grace received at baptism in a conscious act of faith. The fact that baptism is the culminating act in the Roman Catholic Church's *Rite of Christian Initiation for Adults* clearly ties baptism to the Church's task of evangelisation.

- **Sanctification**

  The beginning of sanctification is represented liturgically in baptism. The Eucharist follows as a confirming sacrament that extends and strengthens the sanctifying grace begun in baptism. Growth in grace requires constant, sustained, life-long attention to God and the Lord's Supper is the food that sustains this journey. It is our traveller's provision for our pilgrim journey through life. The invitation to the Lord's Supper has to some extent been replaced in the revivalist tradition by the altar call, so that the Lord's Supper has not been utilised as it might have been as a means for promoting holiness in the corporate setting. It must be noted again here that the origins of the altar call lie in the outdoor sacramental services during the Great Awakenings in America.

- **Anticipation** - a preview of the marriage supper of the Lamb.

  The Lord's Table celebrates our hope in the final restoration of all things to God. We look back to the upper room, where the Lord's Supper was initiated, but also forward to the heavenly banquet where our union with Christ will be consummated. Early church Eucharistic liturgies included both the "upper room" liturgy (looking back) and the "marriage supper" liturgy (looking forward). The second of these has undergone an exciting contemporary renewal.

Here are some practical considerations in preparing for and leading Communion services.

Some Practical Eucharistic Considerations

- Most communion meditations focus almost exclusively on the cross. While this is certainly a proper focus there is no reason why it needs to be the *only* focus. You might do a Bible Study focusing on all references in the Gospels to eating meals, feasts etc.[44] Use your findings as a resource for communion sermons and/or meditations. You will find that there is a wealth of material available that will provide you and your congregation a fresh look at Communion.

- Think of songs and hymns that could be used other than the ones in the hymn book designated as "For the Lord's Supper" and "On the Death of Christ." Why not sing "Christ the Lord is Risen Today," "Rejoice the Lord is King," or "I Know that My Redeemer Lives" as a way of stressing Christ's victory and rule?

- Ask people to *come to the table* rather than be served in their seats. Christ

---

44   A good resource for this is Craig L. Blomberg, *Contagious Holiness: Jesus' Meals with Sinners* (Downers Grove: IVP), 2005.

invites us to his Table. This invitation should elicit a physical response on our part rather than passive inaction.

- Find ways of affirming our unity in Christ, for example the use of a common cup. In many Baptist, Church of Christ and Pentecostal congregations the small communion cups are held until the congregation is ready to drink simultaneously, thus symbolising 'eating and drinking together in the Lord.'

- It is one of the great tragedies of the Church that it is currently divided over the Eucharist. Some Christians cannot participate in the Eucharistic services of churches other than their own without breach of ecclesiastical protocol. As sad as this situation is one must show sensitivity and respect toward the conscience of others. Sometimes a "prayer of blessing" is given instead but this may seem a poor substitute for bread and wine, body and blood. Professor Robert Gribben's practice over a forty year period at the United Faculty of Theology was to bid such persons come forward and then with arms folded across the chest to offer a prayer along the following lines. "Holy God, your Son prayed that we might be one, as you and he are one. Grant by your Holy Spirit that the day may soon come when Christians may eat at the same table on earth, as you promise we shall at your heavenly feast." Such a prayer faces our divisions openly, respects the individual's conscience and takes some kind of action toward healing the current divisions.

- What about children? Should they be permitted to come to the Table and at what age? If children are baptised there seems no compelling reason why they should not be able to approach the Table. Unless your denomination has a regulation about this, it might be best to leave the decision to the parents. In any case, the pastor should model an attitude of welcome for all who would come forward. Pastors should take time with children to train them in the proper manner of receiving Communion – at what point in the service they should come forward, where they should stand, how they should hold their hands, what they should do with the cup, how and when they should return to their seats and so on. Even if parents prefer not to have their young children commune, you might invite them forward for a brief prayer of blessing or a prayer that joyfully anticipates their eventual admission to the Table. By all means find ways of affirming the full participation of children in the life of the church.

I do quite a bit of travelling. During these times I look forward to three things – a refreshing wash, to remove the dust of the road, fellowship around a meal which restores my energies both physically and spiritually, and finally, the good conversation of Christian friends as we share from God's Word and from our own stories of experience with Christ. My hosts bless me in these three ways – with a bath, a meal, and a story. So it is with the sacraments – we are washed from sin, seated at table, and gathered to hear the story of God's great salvation.

Some Questions

1. Have you ever heard somebody say "I'm not sure I'm ready for baptism" as though they believed baptism was a mark of special, advanced commitment rather than something that belonged at the beginning of the Christian life? What reasons might be given for a person holding this belief?

2. Do you agree that parents should be given the option of either baptising or dedicating their children and that pastors should be willing to offer whichever they request? Are there any situations in which it would be wrong for pastors to refuse to either baptise or dedicate an infant?

3. Describe your congregation's typical Communion service and its significance for you.

4. Who should be admitted to the Lord's Table? Does Jesus' practice of "eating with sinners" have any bearing on the answer to this question?

Further Reading:

Burton-Edwards, Taylor. "How Open the Table?: Current Discernment in Three Denominations," *Doxology* Vol. 20 (2003), 40-59.

Gribben, Robert. *Uniting in Thanksgiving: The Great Prayers of Thanksgiving of the Uniting Church in Australia.* Melbourne: Uniting Academic Press, 2008.

Staples, Rob. *Outward Sign, Inward Grace.* Kansas City: Beacon Hill Press, 1991.

Wainwright, Geoffrey. *Eucharist and Eschatology.* London: Epworth Press, 2003.

Willimon, William. *Worship as Pastoral Care.* Nashville: Abingdon, 1994.

CHAPTER ELEVEN

Celebrating Special Days and Seasons: The Church Year

The Christian Year is "an arrangement by which special days and seasons of the year are set aside for the commemoration of particular aspects of the Christian faith."[1] It gradually developed in the early church, and followed the pattern set in the Old Testament, with its ordered round of high festivals and solemn days of remembrance, such as the Passover, the Day of Atonement, the Day of Pentecost, and so on. Some of these were taken over by the Christian Church for its own use. The purpose of the Christian Year is to help us celebrate the great acts of God in salvation in an annual cycle that serves to shape our lives more fully according to the Gospel story, and to respond with thanks for all that God has done. It is yet another way to set forth the sacred narrative of salvation.

The two focal points of the work of salvation are Incarnation and Atonement. The Church Year follows this arrangement with the first part of the year based on the two great festivals of Christmas and Easter, each with a corresponding period of preparation – Advent preparing for Christmas, and Lent preparing for Easter. Pentecost concludes this first half of the year with a stress on the reception of the gift of the Holy Spirit. The second half of the year (the season after Pentecost or ordinary time) is concerned with applying and living out the salvation we have celebrated in the first half.

Advent

The Christian Year begins on the first Sunday of Advent, which is the fourth Sunday before Christmas Day, or the Sunday closest to 31 November. This season bears witness to the "coming" of Christ, both in his humiliation at Bethlehem and in his final glory at the Last Day. It is, therefore, a time of preparation. In fact, it speaks of Christ's coming in a threefold sense 1) the coming of Christ in the flesh, 2) the coming of Christ in Word and Spirit now, 3) the coming of Christ in glory at the end of the age. The colour for Advent is violet.

Why the use of colours for each of the seasons of the church year? It is not certain whether they were chosen arbitrarily or with some specific symbol in

---

1   A.A. Fleming, *The Christian Year* (Iona: Iona Community Publishing), 8. Much of the material in this chapter draws upon Hoyt L. Hickman, Don E. Saliers, Laurence Hull Stookey and James F. White, *The New Handbook of the Christian Year: Based on the Revised Common Lectionary* (Nashville: Abingdon, 1992).

mind. Consciously or unconsciously certain colours are indicative of certain moods and feelings. White is clean and pure and is used in all feasts of Christ; green speaks of growth and of spring. Black suggests darkness, suffering, and death.[2] Red is for blood or fire. In any case, their use in our churches today may serve as one more way of appealing to the senses.[3]

There is a temptation during Advent to sing Christmas carols but it is best if these are held in reserve until the Christmas season when they will then have a much greater impact. However there needs to be pastoral sensitivity toward the congregation. "Shallow pastoral understanding, teaching or leadership can make Advent feel like nothing more that the Christmas Grinch stealing away everybody's holiday fun."[4] Some Evangelical churches don't observe Advent at all, sharing a Puritan distaste for special days. They may perhaps run a Christmas service and leave it at that. To boycott Advent does leave us open to the danger of being swept up into the considerable materialism of the secular Christmas with its jingle bells, and Boxing Day sales. When we say that "the Christ is being taken out of Christmas," we have a tendency to blame those outside the church. But it is often because we have not ourselves done enough to prepare for Christmas in the season of Advent that Christmas loses its uniquely Christian meaning.

Candles are often used during Advent, to stress the coming of Christ who is the "light of the world." Often an Advent wreath is used, containing a candle for each week of Advent and a central "Christ candle" to be lit on Christmas Day. This arrangement is a more recent innovation, considered redundant by some, since the Advent candles speak of anticipating Christ and when Christ has come they lose their relevance.

Christmas

Christmas, the celebration of Christ's birth, did not come into general use until the fourth century. In the wake of the Christological definitions at Nicaea and elsewhere, the stress on the Incarnation of God in the flesh gave rise to its isolation from the earlier season of Epiphany, celebrated by the Eastern Church, during which Christ's birth was celebrated on 6 January. The Western practice of observing 25 December gradually dominated and the Nativity (Christmas) was separated from the season of Epiphany. One symbol

---

2   Of course, to speak of "white" as the colour of purity and "black" as suggesting darkness is not intended to reflect in any way on race or skin colour.

3   Robert Gribben expounds the significance of the colour schemes of the Church Year in "Liturgical Dress in the Uniting Church," http://assembly.uca.org.au/worship/resources/10-guidelines/28-liturgicaldress.html, accessed 2 May 2013.

4   Donald Saliers, *Worship as Theology: Foretaste of Glory Divine* (Nashville: Abingdon, 1994), 20-21.

for Christmas is the IHS – the English transliteration of the first three Greek letters in the name of Jesus. Another appropriate symbol is the Chi Rho the first two Greek letters in the word "Christ" X + P superimposed upon each other.

The symbol of the Lamb of God (*Agnus Dei*) reminds us of John the Baptist as the forerunner of the Messiah as these were the words he used in announcing the coming of Christ - "Here is the Lamb of God who takes away the sin of the world!" (John 1:29) Others symbols include the shepherd's staff, the manger, a candle, the star of Bethlehem, and angels, all relating to the story of the Nativity. Neither the IHS nor the Chi Roh are limited to the Christmas season but are also used widely throughout the year. The colour for Christmas is white and its theme is rejoicing for the gift of God's Son.

Some Christians object to Christmas because of pagan associations with certain Christmas traditions, such as December 25th having once been in ancient times the birthday of the sun, or the Christmas tree being a pre-Christian European symbol of fertility.[5] At other times it's the materialism they object to – all the madness of the silly season, the commercialization and the singing of such theology-lite songs as "Rudolf the Red-Nosed Reindeer." A third objection is an odd one for those concerned for mission, but some complain about those who attend church only at Christmas and Easter and never at any other time of year. We should perhaps remember that the three wise men were pagan magicians – astrologers, magi, dabblers in the occult sciences. But when they saw the Christ child, they worshipped. So there will be many people in church on Christmas Day who haven't been to church since last Christmas. Some of these will see the Christ child and worship him. Whilst protecting the theological integrity of its own rites, the church should also welcome everyone to the manger at Christmas – pagan, Christian, Moslem, atheist – they may all look at this wonderful scene and marvel.

We should resist the temptation to try to control the Christmas season. It isn't necessary that everything that happens be theologically and liturgically watertight. True, there were not three wise men (Scripture speaks only of "wise men" without giving a number), and Jesus wasn't actually born on 25 December. There is a time and a place for getting those factual details right but Christmas is a time to lay aside our scruples and welcome and rejoice with all who come to reflect on the miracle of Christmas. When I served as a pastor in the inner Melbourne suburb of Prahran, Como Park was the site of the annual Carols by Candlelight. Perhaps the biggest event on the City of Stonnington's

---

5   The view that Christmas replaced an earlier pagan festival of the birth of the sun is now doubted by many scholars.

calendar it drew thousands every year. The musical programme would swing from the sublime to the ridiculous – from "O Holy Night" to "Santa Claus is Coming to Town." I learned not to be bothered by this. After all, Jesus came for the foolish as well as the wise - for the three stooges as well as the three wise men. Some of the attendees were Christians, but I would say most were not. These people, young and old, single and married, straight and gay, went on their annual pilgrimage to Carols in the Park to be touched once again by the mystery and the wonder of it all. Advent and Christmas are among those rare times when the Church's liturgical calendar and the activities of the secular world intersect. For that we can choose to be either cynical or thankful. I have tried to opt for the latter.

Epiphany

The thirteenth day after Christmas Day (6 January) is the Feast of the Epiphany, a time to celebrate the *manifestation* of Christ to the nations. Apart from Sunday (which is the oldest and most significant Christian feast) and Easter, this is the oldest festival of the Christian year, but usually the most neglected. The word "epiphany" means "to show forth." It is linked with the story of the Magi in Matthew 2:1-12, and emphasizes the worldwide reach of the Christian revelation.

Before the popularity of Christmas Day, Epiphany was the day on which the church celebrated the birth of Christ. Later it came to be linked instead to Christ's baptism in which he was revealed to the world through his earthly ministry. This was the stress Martin Luther preferred for Epiphany. White is the colour for the Feast of the Epiphany, but green is the colour for the season of Epiphany that follows it (the Sundays *after* Epiphany). This symbolises the new life and hope that Christ brings into the world. It is an appropriate time for a missionary emphasis. Symbols include the star of Bethlehem which guided the magi, an orb representing the world and mounted by a cross, and the baptismal shell with water dripping from it.

Lent

Lent opens on Ash Wednesday and continues until Holy Week, its forty days being a season of fasting and penitence in preparation for the great Easter festival. The imposition of ashes on Ash Wednesday has its ancient origins in the Hebrew practice of fasting and mourning "in sackcloth and ashes." It developed from the period of fasting undertaken by the catechumens in the early church before they were baptized at Easter. No fasting takes place on Sundays not even on the Sundays in Lent since Sunday is never a day of penitence, but is always a "mini-Easter." Since Sundays are not included in Lent it is technically a forty-day period even though it extends over forty-six days. The season is related biblically to Jesus' forty day fast after his baptism when he was led by the Spirit into the wilderness to be tempted by the devil (Luke 4:1-13). This story has overtones of the forty days of fasting by Moses, and by Elijah, and to the forty years spent wandering in the wilderness under Moses. Its name probably comes from the German word *Lenz* and the Anglo-Saxon *lenchthen*, meaning "Spring," a time when the days begin to lengthen. Like Advent, its colour is also violet which speaks both of the royalty of Christ and of his passion. Its message is "Repent of your neglect of and indifference to the things of God. Live close to him so that your faith is renewed." While the cross is an appropriate symbol throughout the Christian year, it takes on special significance during Lent when the readings in the Lectionary take us along with Jesus on his inevitable journey to the cross.

Holy Week

Now we move day by day into the events of the last week of Our Lord's earthly life. Holy Week is an older season than Lent itself, Lent being an extension of it.

Palm Sunday (or Passion Sunday) is the last Sunday before Easter and ushers us into Holy Week. In the Middle Ages this was the Sunday on which the entire story of Christ's passion was read in church, and this practice has been recovered in many churches. Others limit the focus to the entry of the Lord into Jerusalem on that great final week, originally only the beginning of a much longer liturgy. Its symbol is the palm branch.

Maundy Thursday (or Holy Thursday) commemorates the Last Supper and the institution of the Lord's Supper. Its name is derived from the Latin *mandatum* meaning "command" because it was on this night that the Lord "mandated" the "new commandment" that we should love one another as he has loved us (John 13:34). A foot washing service is often held recalling the action of Jesus toward his disciples on that night when he showed them that "he loved them to the end" (13:1) by washing their feet. Grapes and wheat are a common symbol for this day.

Good Friday marks the day of Christ's suffering and death on the cross (his Passion). Its name probably comes from the old English expression "God's Friday," just as "Good-bye" originally meant "God be with ye." Removing all decorations from the sanctuary "seals the tomb" until Sunday. The cross is the primary symbol of Good Friday, often with the INRI lettering representing the Latin inscription *Iesus Nazarenus Rex Iudaeorum* – "Jesus of Nazareth, King of the Jews." Other symbols include the Lamb of God, and the crown of thorns.

Holy Saturday, is observed with a prayer vigil, sometimes until Easter morning when we celebrate Christ's resurrection victory. The colour for Holy Week is red, speaking of Jesus' blood, except for Good Friday when it is replaced by black. The cross remains the major symbol throughout this week.

Easter

Easter is the high point of the Church Year, the greatest of all Christian festivals and the central hub from which the rest of the Christian calendar spreads out and organises itself. Celebrated in the Western church as a moveable feast, it occurs on the first Sunday after the full moon falling upon or after 21 March, which is the first day of Spring in the northern hemisphere. In most of the Eastern churches it is still held according to the Julian calendar (the West follows the Gregorian calendar). It can occur, therefore, anywhere between 22 March and 25 April. Easter was originally called *Pascha*, a word derived from the Hebrew word for "Passover," and so we speak of the "Paschal season," the "Paschal candle" etc.

The connection of Easter with the name of a pagan goddess is a disputed point among historians. Some believe that the word "Easter" comes from the Anglo-Saxon spring goddess, *Eostre*, whose festival coincided with the spring equinox. Since Easter takes place in the northern hemisphere, it came to be applied to the Paschal Feast. Others reject this on the basis that at the time the word first began to be used in the churches of Britain, the church was particularly concerned about the blending of pagan and Christian practice and was trying to keep the church free of all pagan influence. This has led many scholars to doubt that "Easter" had reference to the pagan goddess in its earliest Christian origins, but think rather that is was connected to the earlier and more innocent use of "Spring." Whatever the pagan associations of the word may or may not be it is certainly no longer a pagan word. It is a Christian word now, completely removed from whatever earlier connotations it may once have had, and universally recognised as the greatest of all Christian festivals. Easter, or course, celebrates Christ's glorious resurrection from the dead. Its colour is white. Symbols include the crown of Christ, the empty tomb, the egg, and the butterfly, all of which speak of the new life that Christ brings.

Easter is not a day but a season, a fifty day period that recalls the time spent by the Risen Lord revealing himself to his disciples and to others before ascending to be with his Father and then sending the Spirit upon the waiting disciples. In the medieval period Easter was concluded on Ascension Day, the fortieth day after Easter Sunday, always a Thursday,[6] though the ecumenical consensus is now that it is a fifty day period culminating in Pentecost. Easter

---

6   If a service is not held on Thursday, Ascension can be observed on the following Sunday.

commemorates the Lord's exaltation to the right hand of God and testifies to his present and everlasting rule. The colour for the Easter Season continues as white and the symbol for Ascension is the crown of Christ.

Pentecost

Ten days after Ascension comes the day of Pentecost (or Whitsunday) with a stress on the ministry of the Holy Spirit in the Church. It is associated with the giving of the Law through Moses on Mt. Sinai, understood as the founding of the Jews as a "nation," now freed from captivity in Egypt, and the founding of the Christian Church on the Day of Pentecost with the descent of the Spirit upon the waiting disciples. Red is the colour and the central idea is a life of holiness and empowerment for service and witness. Its symbols are the dove and the flame.

Trinity Sunday

This day bears witness to the Christian doctrine of God as Father, Son, and Holy Spirit. It is an independent feast day and not part of the Easter cycle. It does however usher in the season variously known as Trinity Season, the Season after Pentecost, or simply Ordinary Time. It is a good opportunity to preach on the Trinity, an all too often neglected doctrine in preaching. Its colour is white because it is a feast of Christ, without whom God's triune nature could not be made known to us. Of course, "Whiteness" in connection with Jesus, here and elsewhere, has nothing to do with race or skin colour! It evokes rather his transfiguration when his clothes "became dazzling white, whiter than anyone in the world could bleach them." (Mark 9:2-4) Traditionally the Nicene Creed is recited on this day.

The Season after Pentecost (Ordinary Time)

We have seen that the Christian Year so far is made up of two great cycles – Advent-Christmas-Epiphany followed by Lent-Easter-Pentecost (with Easter the high point of the year). There then follows a long season of "ordinary time" during which we are concerned with the practical outworking of the Christian life. The colour for the Season after Pentecost is green which speaks of growth and renewal. It may be that the choice of green has a more mundane origin, green being the most readily available and least expensive vegetable dye in ancient times.[7] It is called "Ordinary Time" not because these are "ordinary" Sundays but simply because of the numbering of the days (ordinals) – ("1st, 2nd, or 3rd Sunday after Pentecost" or "Pentecost 1, Pentecost 2, Pentecost 3" etc.) This is the longest season of the Christian Year and continues until the very doorstop of Advent when the cycle begins again.

---

7   Robert Gribben, "Liturgical Dress in the Uniting Church," http://assembly.uca.org.au/worship/resources/10-guidelines/28-liturgicaldress.html accessed 30 April 2013.

Christ the King

This is the Last Sunday after Pentecost and the last Sunday of the Christian Year. It is not just an ending however but a transition into the Advent season (which begins the Sunday following) when the whole cycle begins again. Christmas is already looming in people's minds by this time and Christ the King reminds us that is not just the baby in the manger that we welcome but our reigning God. "Joy to the world! The Lord has come. Let earth receive her king!" The celebration of Christ's rule should avoid any note of triumphalism. Romantic, antiquarian and colonial views of human monarchies have no place here. Christ rules as a Servant King and his kingdom is 'not from this world' (John 18:36).

The Value of the Christian Year

The Christian Year is a powerful tool for discipleship, as it aids in holding together in proper proportion a celebration of the great facts and events upon which the Christian life is based. The first part of the year – Advent-Christmas-Lent-Easter-Pentecost- answers the question, "What do Christians believe?" and the second part (the season after Pentecost), "What ought a Christian to do?" The essential principle of the Christian Year, and of liturgy broadly, is not the use of set forms, but the setting forth of the saving acts of God. It places emphasis, as the New Testament itself does, on what God has done – the saving acts of God in Christ, those "once for all" events by which our salvation is accomplished, rather than upon current events, ecclesiastical trends, individual experience, or the preacher's pet peeves. In centering upon what *God* has done it underscores the futility of our own efforts and announces for us a year of grace. Its comprehensive nature ensures that no aspect of the Christian faith and life is untouched and so it addresses every aspect of our spiritual lives.

The Christian Year can serve as an antidote to the heresies and "isms" that often afflict the Church when it forgets the core content of its proclamation and the narrative of salvation is forgotten. It is a practical way that priests and pastors can ensure a balanced all-inclusive teaching program that will feed the mind, the heart, and the senses, with the Grand Story of redemption. It helps us to "sanctify" time. The intrusion of secular holidays into worship (Anzac Day, Mothers' Day, Australia Day etc.) should be guarded against as they tend to obscure God's way of marking time. These secular holidays may be referred to in intercessory prayers, and preachers may choose to address them, but they should never become that which drives the worship service. Similarly while denominational days of special emphasis help us focus on the work of mission, justice, education, evangelism, etc, as far as possible these should flow with, rather than interrupt the Christian Year.

The Christian Year also has eschatological significance. It helps us live "between the times." It involves a rite of separation from fallen, human time - old time - which speaks of our old status and nature, and into sacred time – what it means to be a Christian, who I am in Christ. It then involves a rite of reincorporation into an ordinary time that is no longer "old time" but is now "renewed time." We are reminded of our renewed status as children of God, as the recipients of God's saving and sanctifying grace, and sent back out into ordinary time as those who are *in* the world of old time but not *of* it. Rather we are citizens of God's reign which has already come, is here among us, and yet is still coming. The Christian Year reminds us that a sanctuary for worship exists not only in *space*, but also in *time*.

The Christian Year serves as an effective bridge between the Christian churches, helping us to affirm our unity by following together the same annual pattern of celebration. Sometimes churches hold seasons of prayer and fasting connected with their denominational programmes, resulting in people being forced to fast for two periods of the year, or to miss out on observing either the Lenten fast or the denominationally prescribed one. We should be careful that our "in house" arrangements are not in conflict with or deemed to be of more significance than the faith and practice of the historic church and the theological rationale behind the ordering of the Christian Year. Like most worship resources, the Christian Year is a good servant but a poor master. It should not be considered a noose around our necks or a heavy burden to drag around with us. It is designed to enhance our spirituality and our discipleship. As such it is a time honoured, tested, and proven tool, which we neglect to our own loss.

Some Questions

1. Which of the seasons of the Christian Year does your church currently observe and how are they celebrated?

2. Many Christians are negative toward the commercialism associated with Christmas and Easter and the secularisation they have undergone. What positive opportunities does the widespread celebration of these festivals in the larger community offer for the proclamation of the Gospel?

3. Have you ever fasted during Lent? If so, what was your experience like? If not, do you think there would be any value in doing so?

4. Have you ever attended a foot washing service? What issues would

need to be considered in planning such an observation?

5. Do you agree with the late Robert Webber that Evangelical and Charismatic churches must consider adopting the Christian calendar? Why or why not?

Further Reading:

Brown, Raymond. *Christ in the Gospels of the Liturgical Year*. Collegeville, MN: Liturgical Press, 2008.

Hickman, Hoyt L., Don E. Saliers, Laurence Hull Stookey and James F. White, *The New Handbook of the Christian Year: Based on the Revised Common Lectionary*. Nashville: Abingdon, 1992.

Stookey, Lawrence Hull. *Calendar: Christ's Time for the Church*. Nashville: Abingdon, 1996.

Webber, Robert. *Ancient-Future Time: Forming Spirituality through the Christian Year*. Grand Rapids: Baker, 2004.

Some Internet Resources

The Text This Week http://www.textweek.com/

The Laughing Bird - Resources for Christian Worship with an Australian Accent http://www.laughingbird.net/LaughingBird/Welcome.html

Worship Homepage of the United Methodist Church's General Board of Discipleship http://www.gbod.org/worship/

Chapter Twelve

Putting it All Together: Preparing a Worship Service

We now need to think about the actual preparation and leading of worship services. All of the theology and history that we have studied should be the foundation for the planning and leading of worship services. A good worship service will either follow a theme, such as one provided by the Christian Year, or by the sermon text. This provides the internal logic for the selection of songs, readings, prayers, and other actions of the service.

Once this theme is established, a good place to begin in constructing the shape of the service is to return to the very first chapter and consider the fourfold shape of the liturgy and its movements

- Assembling the people (Gathering)
- Scripture reading and preaching (The Service of the Word)
- Response to the Word (Holy Communion or other acts of thanksgiving)
- Sending the people forth (Dismissal)

As we consider each of these points in turn suggestions for planning and also for the actual leadership of the service will be more or less intermingled together. There are many excellent resources available for constructing worship services so by all means do an Internet search to track down resources. Mainline denominational sites are good because they are designed to service congregations that are using the Lectionary readings and following the services of the Christian Year.

The Gathering

In one sense the service will have begun in the vestry where you have drawn aside for a quiet period of prayerful reflection before the service begins. The public commencement of the service must then begin with a definite beginning. People need a clear signal that the liturgy is now commencing. If there is a musical prelude of some sort this may help people be alert to the fact that the service is about to begin. At the conclusion of this, move decisively forward to a central point and give a greeting in a clear and distinct voice. You should not shout but you must project your voice so that all may hear. If your greeting requires a response, make sure that the congregation is clear on what the response is to be. For example if the greeting is "The Lord be with you," you must have the appropriate response - "And also with you" - on the data projector or inserted in a church bulletin or other handout. What you say must match with what is written or a great deal of confusion will result. A seasoned congregation will know such responses off by heart but if you are introducing such responses as something new you will need to do some coaching.

Keep in mind the distinction here between a "Call to Worship" and an "Invocation." The first addresses the people, therefore you should maintain good eye contact with the congregation and, if possible, memorise your greeting. The second, on the other hand, addresses God, so you should invite people to join you in prayer. Of course, you may have both a Call to Worship and an Invocation, but if you do this make sure the Call to Worship comes first. If you are following a set liturgy keyed to the Church Year and the Lectionary, calls to worship and other "sentences" will be chosen for you already. If not, there are many Psalms that can serve as excellent calls to worship. One often used is Psalm 95:6-7 "O Come, let us worship and bow down, let us kneel before the Lord our Maker! For he is our God and we are the people of his pasture, and the sheep of his hand."

Your overall demeanour during the whole service, the tone of which must be set in these opening moments, should be a balance of reverence and enthusiasm. You do not wish to be sombre (you are not at a funeral), but on the other hand you should not try to get the congregation "on side" by attempting to be funny, or by being overly casual and friendly. You are aware of the dignity of worship and at the same time you are enthusiastic to be there, passionate about God and the Gospel and glad to have the privilege of leading God's people in worship. The last thing you want to do is look bored!

It is best if the opening hymn or song focuses on the greatness of God and be a song of worship rather than of testimony. Testimony songs belong more naturally during the time of Response and Thanksgiving. Here in the early part of the service we want to look upward to God who is worthy of our praise and into whose Holy Presence we have come. You may draw upon your church's hymnbook or other music resources. Never introduce a song that is new to the congregation during this movement of the service. You need a song that is well known to all, or at least to most, so that the proper note of confident praise can be struck. You are setting a tone for the rest of the service and you do not want to get off to an uncertain start from which it may prove difficult to recover.

If you gave a call to worship earlier, rather than an invocation, a good place for your opening prayer is at the conclusion of this opening song. This should be brief and to the point. It is not a time for intercessory prayer (praying for the sick, or the absent, or for world peace), but to address God and commit the time of worship into God's hands. If you have already given a Prayer of Invocation do not muddy the waters by offering a second prayer at this point. Simply move on to further songs of praise or move straight into the Service of the Word.

The Service of the Word

Churches that use a set Lectionary of texts will already have four readings available to them, which saves a great deal of time and trouble in selection. These will be a Psalm (perhaps already used during the Gathering), an Old Testament reading (except during the Easter Season when this is replaced by a reading from the Book of Acts), an Epistle Reading, and a Gospel Reading. One of these texts will be the sermon text for the day, or perhaps a sermon may be built by reflecting upon all four. In this way the theme of the service is decided for you.

If you have chosen the texts yourself, you will want to ensure that they have some logical and theological connection with each other. You may not wish to have four readings, but I suggest you should have at least two – one from each of the two Testaments. These may simply be read in a block or be punctuated by spoken responses, songs, or creedal affirmations. The following is a contemporary affirmation used at Spring Street Wesleyan Methodist Church, Prahran as a response to the Scripture readings.

A KINGDOM AFFIRMATION

Pastor: Wherever the Risen Christ is present,
In the midst of the worshipping community,
There is the one true church, apostolic and universal;
Whose holy faith we now declare:
Pastor and People:
We believe in God the Father,
Infinite in wisdom, power, and love,
Whose mercy is new every morning,
Who delivers the poor and needy,
And whose lovingkindness is over all his works.
We believe in Jesus Christ,
Son of God and Son of Man,
Saviour of the World,
He embodied the Kingdom,
Preached forgiveness,
Healed the sick,
Raised the dead,
And ate with sinners.

We believe in the Holy Spirit,
The breath of God,
Who gives new life,
Who makes holy,
Who gives us life and sustains our lives,
Who with the Father and the Son is One God forever
We believe that this faith should be expressed,
In the love of God and neighbour,
In welcoming the alien and the stranger,
In personal faith and social action,
In opposition to evil,
In cultivation of the good,
And in hope of the world to come.
Amen

In some churches the congregation stands for the reading of the Gospel. This does not mean that the Gospels are more inspired than other parts of the Bible. Rather, it symbolises the centrality of the Gospels since the Old Testament points towards the events recorded there and the Epistles are a kind of commentary upon them. It adds reverence to the reading to carefully announce the passage in suitable words, such as "Hear the Word of the Lord in the Gospel according to St. John," or even simply, "Today's Epistle reading is taken from the Letter to the Hebrews, chapter 10, and verse 3." Remember to give people time to find the passage in their Bibles if they wish, though the best posture for the congregation is to look up into the face of the reader and quite literally, *hear* the Word of the Lord.

Also, suitable closing words are important, so as not to leave the passage "hanging." For example, "The Word of God for the people of God," or "This is the Word of the Lord," to which the congregation replies, "Thanks be to God." The proper closing words after the Gospel are "This is the Gospel of Our Lord Jesus Christ." For a simpler, less formal closing, try "May God add his blessing to the reading of his Word," to which the people may simply reply, "Amen."

It is a special honour to read God's Word for God's people, and we should approach it with reverence, as ministry. Reading the Bible in the context of the church's liturgy is as old as the church itself and the early church actually "ordained" lectors. In the reading of the Bible, preparation is essential.[1] Readers emphasise words wrongly when they have not done the pre-reading required to understand the meaning of what they read. The wrong emphasis can confuse or even completely change the meaning of what is read.

---

1   For a little booklet full of practical advice see Clifford Warne and Paul White, *How to Read the Bible Aloud* (Sydney: AIO Press, 1986).

In addition to emphasis, phrasing is also important. One should read neither too fast nor too slow. When people are nervous they tend to read too fast. You may want to deliberately force yourself to slow down to counteract this tendency. Pauses help make the meaning of the passage clear and give the congregation time to let the reading sink in. They also draw attention to thoughts and ideas that might otherwise be missed. Actors call the printed word "the text." They know that the audience does not come to the theatre to hear them simply *say* the text. They are wanting the actors to reveal the subtext – the *undermeaning* – how the words should be spoken so as to reveal their true meaning. Sometimes the biblical authors provide us with the "undermeaning" of a passage (John 12:5, Luke 9:33). Usually, however, we have to do a little research to discover it for ourselves. This may mean consulting a commentary or at least the footnotes in a Study Bible.

This is not a book about preaching but since a sermon or homily is part of almost every worship service it may be helpful to provide a brief homiletical model here. In interpreting a text in preparation for preaching, ask three questions of the text.

- What does the text *say*? (This is simply a matter of careful observation.)
- What does the text *mean*? (Here we move beyond observation to interpretation.)
- How do I *apply* the text to myself and my hearers? (The important final step of application.)

Once you are able to answer these three questions write an outline of your talk something like the following

- Introduction - an opening illustration that both introduces the point of the text and gains your hearer's attention.
- Point 1 – with brief illustration (a quote, an incident, an anecdote, a story).
- Point 2 – with a brief illustration.
- Point 3 - with a brief illustration.
- Conclusion – recap, revise, or return to your original illustration to bring the talk full circle, and make an application (what should your hearers now do in light of this word?)

A brief Prayer for Illumination before the sermon asking the Holy Spirit to open up the meaning of the Scripture passage is always appropriate.

The Service of the Table

Once the Word of God has been heard, it needs to be responded to. In a full service of Word and Table the most appropriate response is the Eucharistic celebration. If this is not the case, other acts of thanksgiving and response should be included here – prayers of intercession, invitation to the altar, the offering, baptisms and confirmations are all appropriate. Since different traditions have different rules about who can preside at Communion, I would suggest that if you are constructing this service for a classroom exercise you only choose to lead Communion if the church to which you belong has authorised you to do so. If you are not ordained, some fellow students may prefer not to receive Communion in class. However, you should check with your teacher and be guided by him or her at this point.

If choosing to lead Communion you may either use a printed liturgy or take a "free style" approach.[2] If you would like a second person to work with you as you preside, please communicate with that person and make roles clear. Some congregations practice "'intinction,'" i.e. using a common cup and dipping the individual portions of bread into the cup. If you adopt this practice, having another person hold the bread or the cup as you serve is very helpful. Servers should tilt the cup forward toward the communicant to provide a shallow portion and avoid dipping the fingers into the wine.

While a variety of approaches to the celebration of the Lord's Supper is encouraged, there remains the need to be faithful to the core biblical material and to our Lord's command. In order to preserve this faithfulness it is expected that some form of the "words of institution" (1 Corinthians 11:23b-25) be used. The fourfold action of *taking* (the bread and cup), *thanking* (God for it), *breaking* (the bread), and *giving* (to the people) is at the core of all Eucharistic celebration. This provides a more Christ-centred and biblically-based model than other approaches, but again the exact form of the service will rest, to some extent, with each presider. Asking people to come forward is important as it gives an opportunity for the members of the congregation to reach out to receive the grace of God being offered. You could ask the people to stand in a semi-circular fashion around the table, or they may approach the table single file (this is good in particularly large groups where it is impossible to gather all together in one spot).

If you are preparing for a liturgy class, it is likely (though not inevitable) that all your fellow students and your lecturer will be committed Christians, but in a congregational setting this will not always be the case. You must make clear to people what your practice is in the invitation. If you have an "open table,"

---

2   Part 3 of *Uniting in Thanksgiving* provides invaluable practical advice for those using the Uniting Church's "Great Prayer of Thanksgiving." Gribben, *Uniting in Thanksgiving,* 175-222.

believing that God's love reaches to all and that we are present at his table by the invitation of Christ himself rather than by the invitation or permission of the church, then make that clear. If other conditions apply these need to be made known, though this should be done with sensitivity and tact so as not to send a message of exclusion. You may wish to make it clear to people that they should come to the table if they love and know Christ or if they are *seeking* to love and know him. Or you may wish to set forth baptism as a prerequisite. Once you have set whatever limitations you feel conscience-bound to set, the resulting response must be left between God and the communicant.

When serving the people you may use simple words such as "The body of Christ" or "The body of Christ given for you." You may also preface the giving with words addressed to the whole congregation such as "The body and blood of our Lord Jesus Christ, which was given for you, preserve your soul and body unto everlasting life," or "Take and eat this in remembrance that Christ died for you; Feed on him in your heart, by faith, with thanksgiving." Allow some time for silent reflection and prayer. You might invite people to pray out loud, after which you could conclude with the Lord's Prayer spoken together.

The Dismissal

The final movement of the service sends people out to serve God in the world. It may include such elements as the announcements, since they reflect on what the church will be doing in its mission between Sundays, a closing hymn, a final prayer, and/or a benediction. Remember a Closing Prayer is addressed to God but a Benediction is addressed to the people, so decide which you are going to give (or whether you will give both) and then use the appropriate action. As noted earlier, a Benediction should be given with eyes to the congregation (and received with eyes opened) and with upraised hands in a bountiful gesture of blessing. Numerous scriptural benedictions are available in the Bible.[3] You may use these or compose your own, tying together the themes of the service and/or the sermon. Generally speaking, it is good to master the time-honoured scriptural ones first, committing them to memory, before going on, if you wish, to construct some of your own. Make sure that the "Amen" of the benediction is the very last thing you say. Any words said after the Benediction will take away from its power and dissipate its energy.

Instead of questions or further reading this chapter ends with an invitation for you to construct an order of service. Spend some time writing a liturgy drawing on all that you have learned so far. The Appendix that follows is an evaluation form that will show you what elements you should be including.

---

3   Examples include Numbers 6:24-26, Hebrews 13:20-21, 2 John 3, Galatians 1:3-5, 2 Corinthians 13:14, 2 Thessalonians 34:16,18, 2 Timothy 4:22, Romans 15:5-6, Romans 15:13, 33, Revelatio

.

Evaluating the Worship Service

This template is designed for use in a classroom setting or when evaluating worship serves attended for the purposes of assessment. Remember during these times of worship, that though you are in a "workshop" atmosphere, engaged in a learning experience, you are also actually worshipping God. As you critique your fellow students in the classroom setting do so with grace. First tell the student the things that helped you to worship before going on to suggest ways they may have done better. By all means be honest, but express the truth in love.[1]

General questions:

1. Was God truly worshipped in this service? How so or why not?
2. What was the dominant theme of the service, and what was the value of the truth being conveyed?
3. To what degree, and how, did the service utilise Scripture?
4. To what degree, and how did the serviced involve members of the congregation?

Questions relating to the shape of the liturgy:

1. Did the Gathering involve a clear, attention getting beginning with a call to worship and/or an invocation?
2. Were the four movements of Gathering, Hearing, Responding, and Dismissal clearly observable and was there a smooth transition between them?
3. Was an opportunity given to respond to God's Word?
4. Was the end of the service marked clearly by a closing prayer and/or a benediction?
5. How did this service speak to you personally?

Questions related to the leader:

1. Did the leader seem confident and enthusiastic, or did he/she seem bored or otherwise distracted?
2. Were there any flaws in grammar? What about vocabulary? Did the leader use words well?

---

1   For an alternative evaluation form see Appendix D in Burns, *Pilgrim People*, 217-18.

3. Was the leader's voice easy to listen to? Did he or she express variation in tone? Could the speakers be clearly heard, so as to be understood?

4. Were bodily gestures appropriate? Did the liturgical action match the truth being set forth?

5. What about eye contact? Did the liturgist connect with the hearers in this way?

Lightning Source UK Ltd.
Milton Keynes UK
UKHW051854090919
349467UK00023B/599/P